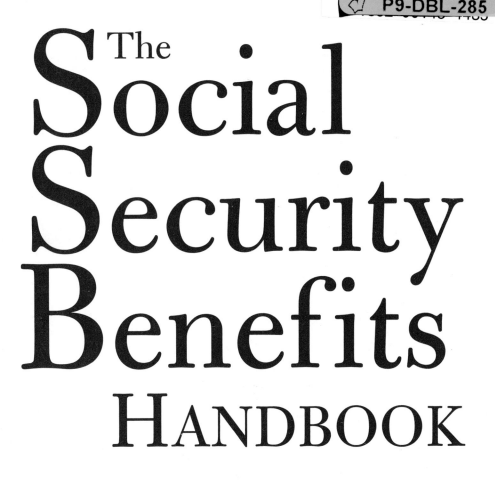

The Social Security Benefits HANDBOOK

5th Edition

Stanley A. Tomkiel III
Attorney at Law

SPHINX® PUBLISHING
AN IMPRINT OF SOURCEBOOKS, INC.®
NAPERVILLE, ILLINOIS
www.SphinxLegal.com

Fifth Edition: 2008

Published by: **Sphinx® Publishing, An Imprint of Sourcebooks, Inc.®**

Naperville Office
P.O. Box 4410
Naperville, Illinois 60567-4410
630-961-3900
Fax: 630-961-2168
www.sourcebooks.com
www.SphinxLegal.com

This publication is designed to provide accurate and authoritative information in regard to the subject matter covered. It is sold with the understanding that the publisher is not engaged in rendering legal, accounting, or other professional service. If legal advice or other expert assistance is required, the services of a competent professional person should be sought.

From a Declaration of Principles Jointly Adopted by a Committee of the American Bar Association and a Committee of Publishers and Associations

This product is not a substitute for legal advice.
Disclaimer required by Texas statutes.

Library of Congress Cataloging-in-Publication Data
Tomkiel, Stanley A.
    The social security benefits handbook / by Stanley A. Tomkiel. -- 5th ed.
        p. cm.
    Includes index.
    ISBN-13: 978-1-57248-577-8 (pbk. : alk. paper)
    ISBN-10: 1-57248-577-9 (pbk. : alk. paper)
    1. Social security--Law and legislation--United States--Popular works. I. Title.
KF3650.T65 2007
344.7302'3--dc22
                                            2006038373

Printed and bound in the United States of America.
SB — 10 9 8 7 6 5 4 3 2 1

CONTENTS

Introduction

The Social Security program in the United States is a massive system of complex and complicated laws, rules, and bureaucracies. Confusion and frustration await people looking for a quick and easy way to access accurate and specific information about Social Security benefits.

Although the Social Security Administration (SSA) provides the public with information and advice about the programs it administers, the reality is, despite its best efforts, many people find it difficult to get the particular information they need, or even to know what they need. And some things are purposely not disseminated, such as SSA's guidelines on accepting compromise offers to settle overpayments (see Section (Sec.) 1110), your right to file only for Medicare without filing for retirement benefits (see Sec. 404.2—sometimes this is beneficial), or your option to prorate work deductions instead of full withholding of benefits (see Sec. 803.1).

The system is complex, with many variables. A bare statement of rules, without practical examples of how they apply in specific cases, is inadequate. Frequently, generalizations are not helpful. Even though it is often beneficial to file for benefits three months in advance of retirement, some people may actually lose some benefits. (see Sec. 404.1.) Even though this rule of thumb applies in many cases, it is small consolation if you lose thousands of dollars by following it.

Sometimes the realities of how the system works do not fit in with the official policies of how it should work. SSA usually does an admirable job. We have included practical information for common problems that beneficiaries confront, such as what to do if checks don't come (see Sec. 1011), if you have to wait for hours to speak with someone (see Sec. 105), if interviewers are incompetent or inexperienced, or if Social Security wants erroneously paid benefits to be returned. (see Chapter 11.) Certainly these things happen in only a relatively small number of cases, but if yours is one of them, you need some practical advice. You are not likely to find it in a pamphlet.

This handbook was designed to give you all the major rules about Social Security benefits:

- to show you how they work in particular cases;

- to highlight the situations that can make a dollars-and-cents difference, or are often misunderstood; and,

- to give you the benefit of my practical experience in dealing with thousands of cases as a "front line" Social Security official.

The handbook contains fourteen chapters by topic, divided into more than two hundred numbered and captioned sections for easy access to specific information, with numerous cross-references and examples for better understanding. It covers just about everything you need to know about monthly benefits.

Hopefully this book will save you time, frustration, and perhaps even some money. The *Social Security Benefits Handbook* will give you a unique understanding and serve as a handy reference source for accurate, substantial, and practical knowledge about this very important part of your life.

Because Social Security rules change periodically, you may find updated information arranged according to the chapter and section structure of this book at the author's website at **www.socialsecuritybenefitshandbook.com**.

THE SOCIAL SECURITY ADMINISTRATION

1

SECTION 101 THE SOCIAL SECURITY ADMINISTRATION—IN GENERAL

The Social Security Administration (SSA) is the branch of the federal government that has the duty of administering several provisions of the *Social Security Act*. The Social Security Administration was under the jurisdiction of the Department of Health and Human Services until March 1995, when it became an independent agency. The Social Security Administration is one of the largest government agencies in the country. The Social Security Act provides for the payment of monthly benefits to retired and disabled workers and their dependents, and to certain survivors of covered workers who are deceased. Social Security also provides for Medicare and other programs such as Supplemental Security Income and Black Lung benefits. The benefits referred to as Social Security benefits, however, are those monthly benefits payable to retired workers, disabled workers, and the survivors of covered workers. Because regular Social Security benefits are based on the earnings of covered workers, the SSA also keeps track of the earnings of almost all American workers.

The SSA pays $43 billion each month to 48 million people throughout the United States. There are 159 million covered workers whose wages are recorded by the Social Security Administration each year. For each beneficiary receiving a check, there are 3.7 workers paying taxes. These workers and their employers pay $580 billion to the government for Social Security taxes. Taxes are collected by the Internal Revenue Service and then reported by the IRS to the SSA.

The SSA is divided into many different bureaus and branches to accomplish all of its duties. The main offices are located in Baltimore, Maryland. The SSA divides the entire United States into districts and each has its own district office. Many of these district offices also have branch offices. There are over 1,300 district and branch offices (collectively called *field offices*) throughout the nation. The district office is designed to handle all contact with members of the public. Most dealings you may have with the SSA will normally be done through your local district office.

This chapter discusses the different bureaus, their general functions, and the different types of district office employees with whom you will come in contact.

SECTION 102 INTERNAL OFFICES

The Social Security Administration makes contact with members of the public through district offices and Teleservice Centers. (see Sec. 103 and Sec. 105.) However, much of the work of the SSA is done by people in offices who have no contact with the public. These internal offices are some that never come into the public view.

Central Office (CO)

The main office of the SSA is called the *Central Office* (CO). It is the headquarters of the SSA and is located in Baltimore, Maryland. The Central Office issues all regulations and instructions to the district offices. It interprets the law and issues policy statements.

Office of Central Records Operations

The *Office of Central Records Operations* (OCRO) deals with the huge volume of information necessary to perform the duties of the Social Security Administration. Its main functions include the assigning of Social Security numbers to workers, keeping track of changes of names on Social Security records, and maintaining the records of earnings reported by employers for each individual Social Security number. This office is also located in Baltimore, Maryland. When a person files a claim for Social Security benefits, the district office where the claim is being handled must contact the Office of Central Records Operations to obtain the earnings record of the worker.

Program Service Centers

There are six *Program Service Centers* (PSCs) located throughout the United States. These offices process claims that cannot be processed by the district office. The PSCs also process reinstatement of benefits after they have been suspended or terminated. After a claim has been processed in a district office, it is sent to the Program Service Center for storage and further processing. The claims folders are generally assigned to the different Program Service Centers, based on the Social Security number of the person on whose earnings the claim is based. Sometimes the Program Service Center will have direct contact with beneficiaries. The PSC handles things such as student reports, annual reports of earnings, and over-payment notices. Any information requested from a Program Service Center can be returned directly or can be returned through a local district office, whichever is preferred.

Office of Disability Operations

The *Office of Disability Operations* (ODO) is similar to a Program Service Center, but it handles cases of disability benefits. A disabled worker, age 59 or older, has his or her file maintained in the Program Service Center instead of the Office of Disability Operations. The files of disabled workers *under* age fifty-nine are kept in the Office of Disability Operations. This office is located in Baltimore, Maryland.

When the person turns 65, his or her disability benefit is automatically converted to a retirement benefit by the Program Service Center. This conversion to a retirement benefit is only a technicality, as the amount of the benefit does not change.

Division of International Operations

The *Division of International Operations* (DIO) is similar to the Program Service Center, but it covers cases where beneficiaries reside outside of the United States. It is also located in Baltimore, Maryland.

Regional Offices

The entire United States is divided into ten regions by the Social Security Administration. Each region has a *regional office* (RO) that deals directly with the Central Office, and then deals with the local district offices within the region. An individual district office in the region does not have direct contact with the Central Office. Instead, it deals through its regional office. The regional office is staffed with experts in all areas of Social Security. Regional offices also review the district offices to make sure that they are applying the rules and regulations of Social Security consistently.

SECTION 103 TELEPHONE SERVICES

The Social Security Administration has set up special centers designed to handle telephone inquiries from members of the public. These are called *Teleservice Centers* (TSC). They are designed to take the burden of voluminous phone calls away from the district office. The nationwide toll-free number is 800-772-1213. Service representatives handle calls from 7 a.m. to 7 p.m. on business days, with prerecorded information and automated services available after hours. Between 7 a.m. and 7 p.m., hearing impaired callers with TDD equipment can call 800-325-0778. Medicare information is available from 8 a.m. to 8 p.m. Eastern time at 800-MEDICARE (800-633-4227). The telephone service is busiest in the early part of the week and the early part of the month—you will get through quicker if you call at other times.

The Teleservice Centers are staffed by service representatives. They have computer terminals available to obtain the computer records of all beneficiaries who have claims that have been established on the computer. They are able to handle changes of address and reports of missing checks. If a claim has been recently filed and has not yet been set up on the computer system, you will be referred to the local district office where the claim is being handled. That phone number is given to you, at the time you filed your initial application, on the receipt form that the SSA gives everyone who files a claim. The Teleservice Centers can also provide general information about Social Security, although it is recommended that you speak with a claims representative if the question is more involved.

District Office Telephone Service

Many district offices have telephone services available to file claims, to report changes of address or missing checks, and to obtain information regarding Social Security. Almost all business you may have with the Social Security office can be handled over the telephone. You can even file a claim over the phone. Many district offices have what is referred to as a *teleclaims unit*. These units are staffed by claims representatives who will obtain the necessary information from you over the phone, complete the application form, and mail it to you for your review and signature.

SOCIAL SECURITY TIP

It is against the policy of many Social Security offices to send out blank application forms.

If you call them up to file a claim, you will have to give the information over the phone so that the claims representative can properly fill out the application. This is done to ensure that there is no misunderstanding of information and that all the information and required evidence is obtained.

SECTION 104 INTERNET WEBSITE

The official Social Security website is found at **www.ssa.gov.** It is comprehensive with many links. You can get a benefit estimate, request a statement of your Social Security record, and even apply for most types of benefits online. You can quickly get access to research data and reports, forms, program rules, regulations, statutes, and rulings. You can even put in your zip code and find the nearest field office.

You must be fairly comfortable working with computers and the Internet to take advantage of these services. Because the official website is so comprehensive, many users may be overwhelmed.

Example: A search for "amount of benefits" returns over fifteen pages of results, each with twenty links to administrative rulings, actuarial data, projections of replacements rates, and much more information that is very useful to sophisticated users.

Because so much information is available, it may take some time and effort to hone in on just what you are looking for.

NOTE: *There is a separate website for Medicare information found at www.medicare.gov.*

SOCIAL SECURITY TIP

For those who are looking for quicker access to basic information in the format in which this book is arranged, visit the online version at:
www.socialsecuritybenefitshandbook.com

SECTION 105 FIELD OFFICES

There are over 1,300 district and branch offices throughout the United States. Each district or branch office is responsible for dealing with all members of the public who reside in that district. Any business you may have to conduct with the SSA will be done through your local district office. You may determine where your district office is located by looking in the telephone book under "United States Government, Social Security Administration;" by calling the nationwide toll-free number; or by going online. You may deal with any district office you prefer. District offices are open during regular business hours, but the exact times of opening and closing change from one office to another. Some offices open at 8:00 a.m. and close at 4:30 p.m., while other offices open at 8:30 a.m. and close at 5:00 p.m. Most of your business with the Social Security Administration can be conducted over the telephone or online.

SOCIAL SECURITY TIP

If you wish to visit your district office in person, usually you *cannot* make an appointment. Visitors at the district office are taken on a first-come, first-served basis.

Visiting the District Office

The volume of visitors to district offices usually follows a pattern. Generally speaking, you are better off going to your district office toward the end of a month. The first week to ten days is usually the busiest. It is at these times that you may encounter a wait of an hour or more. The latter part of the week is typically less busy than the early part of the week— Mondays are usually very busy, whereas Fridays are slow.

The district offices are normally busy during lunchtime. This is because many people who work go there during their lunchtime; while at the same time, the Social Security employees have to eat, too. Interviewers at the Social Security office have staggered lunch hours so that at least half of them will be on duty during this time. However, because the other half is out to lunch, the lines can grow and you may encounter delays. Similarly, the employees at the district office receive coffee breaks—one in the morning and another in the afternoon. Again, these breaks are staggered, but at around 10:00 a.m. and around 3:00 p.m., half of the interviewers are on their coffee breaks.

Processing Units

The business handled by the district office is divided into different units. Each unit is staffed by one or more employees. Among interviewers, the basic division is between claims units and service units. Claims units handle initial applications and the more complex areas of Social Security rules. They are staffed by claims representatives. The service units handle what are referred to as *postentitlement* issues. These are the events that occur after you have become entitled to checks, such as changes of address, reports of missing checks, annual reports of earnings, and so forth. Service units are staffed by service representatives. A service representative is not able to handle an initial claim.

There is typically a special unit set up in each district office to handle disability-related cases and another special unit for Supplemental Security Income cases. (see Sec. 1401.) In larger offices, the work will be further divided among the claims representatives and service representatives based on an alphabetical breakdown.

Each claims representative and service representative will be assigned a certain part of the alphabet and the cases of all persons with last names that fall within that part of the alphabet will be assigned to that particular representative. That worker will handle the paperwork for the claim, but may interview people visiting the district office regardless of the alphabetical breakdown.

SOCIAL SECURITY TIP

Representatives are periodically reassigned to different alphabetical breakdowns, so do not be surprised to find that a different representative is handling your case a few months later.

Branch Offices and Contact Stations

In addition to district offices, the Social Security Administration also sets up *branch offices* and *contact stations.* The branch office is a smaller version of the district office and comes under its jurisdiction. It is staffed with the same types of employees found in the district office. The manager of a branch office reports to the manager of the district office with which it is associated.

The contact station is not a regular office. It is simply a place where a field representative or a claims representative will go on a periodic basis to service people in outlying areas. They are usually set up in areas where the district office has a large juris-diction. The field representative will go to the contact station at set times, such as the third Tuesday of the month. All paperwork is taken back to the district office and processed there by the regular personnel according to the alphabetic breakdown.

If you live far from your local district office, you should find out if a contact station is set up closer to you and if so, when the Social Security representative will be there. Contact stations are commonly established in municipal buildings or senior citizen centers.

SECTION 106 DISTRICT OFFICE PERSONNEL

Each district office is staffed with many different types of employees, each one handling specific functions. Every district office has a *district manager* who is the highest authority in the office. He or she is not usually involved with the technical aspects of the cases, such as deciding claims. The manager's duties are basically administrative, such as maintaining personnel records and making sure the office work moves along quickly. He or she also deals with congresspeople and senators who make inquiries on behalf of their constituents. (see Sec. 1014.) The district manager is the person to contact in the district office if you wish to praise a particular employee for a job well done or to complain about an employee for poor service.

The district manager does not deal with the public on a regular basis. The employees who deal with the public regu-larly are claims representatives, service representatives, field representatives, and the receptionist. In addition to these personnel, there are supervisors, clerical staff, and technical employees who deal with the paperwork and the computers. If you visit your local Social Security office and have to wait because all the interviewers are tied up interviewing people, you may see employees sitting at desks not interviewing anyone. Do not be upset—these are probably the noninterviewing personnel.

Claims Representative

The *claims representative* position is perhaps the single most important position in the Social Security organization. It is the responsibility of the claims representative to be knowledgeable about all aspects of the Social Security regulations. The duty of the claims representative has two sides. One is to represent the Social Security Administration and the other is to assist claimants who are making claims for benefits under the Social Security program. The major responsibility of the claims representative has to do with initial claims for benefits. The claims representative interviews a prospective claimant, determines the type of claim that should be made, and completes the appropriate claims forms.

The claims representative also determines what documents, evidence, or other information is required to successfully prosecute the claim and advises the claimant accordingly. The claims representative also will take steps to obtain the necessary information or documents. Additionally, on many of these initial claims, the claims representative makes the decision to pay or to deny the claim. Along with these duties, the claims representative is also responsible for making determinations relating to representative payees (see Sec. 1414) for incompetent beneficiaries, for making determinations of the proper amount of wages subject to Social Security, and for making recommendations about whether or not overpayments may be waived in particular cases. It is also the duty of the claims representative to provide the public with information about the Social Security rules, regulations, and procedures.

In theory, the claims representative knows everything about the various aspects of Social Security. This knowledge is not gained in a short period of time, however, and in a given district office there will be claims representatives with varying degrees of experience. A person who becomes a claims representative is considered to be a trainee for three years, because it takes at least that long to get a good working knowledge of all the rules and regulations involved with the job. It takes at least another year of experience to become fully versed in all the aspects of Social Security for which the claims representative is responsible.

The majority of seasoned claims representatives are thoroughly knowledgeable professionals who are well versed in all aspects of Social Security laws and regulations. There are some exceptions to that statement—because of the very complex and technical nature of the area, a number of claims representatives, even though they are on the job for many years, are still not completely competent. Just as there are incompetent doctors and lawyers, there are incompetent claims representatives. If you believe that the claims representative you are dealing with is giving you erroneous or inaccurate information, ask to be shown in the *Programs Operations Manual* the authority for his or her statement. (see Sec. 107.) If you are still not satisfied, you should then ask to speak to an operations supervisor to double check.

Service Representative

The *service representative* deals with *postentitlement* aspects—the things that affect people who are already receiving benefits. Service representatives do not handle claims, payee determinations, changes to the earnings record, or other complex areas of Social Security.

The most common matters that a service representative deals with include changes of address, reports of missing checks, annual reports of earnings, refunds of overpayments, and Medicare claims. These employees are also well versed in the *retirement test*, also known as the *earnings limitations rules*. (The retirement test is used to determine how earnings affect benefits and is fully discussed in Chapter 8.)

The workload in a district office is divided among the service representatives according to an alphabetical breakdown. Beneficiaries are assigned to service representatives based on their last names. The service representatives are periodically reassigned to different alphabetical breakdowns. You may not always have the same service representative assigned to your case each time you go to the district office. The alphabetical breakdowns are used only for paperwork processing. Interviewers may be assigned without regard to alphabetical breakdowns if this is required to avoid delays.

The job of the service representative requires a thorough knowledge of complicated rules and procedures. Most service representatives are very competent. Unfortunately, some are not. If you question the accuracy of information or advice from a service representative, you should ask him or her to show you the authority for the information in the Claims Manual or Programs Operations Manual. (see Sec. 107.) If you are still not satisfied, you may ask to speak to an operations supervisor.

Field Representative

Each district and branch office has at least one *field representative*. A field representative is a claims representative who goes out of the office when the need arises. This usually occurs when a claimant or beneficiary is homebound or in a hospital. The field representative makes speeches before groups and visits contact stations. The field representative does not usually process the paperwork personally. He or she brings it back to the district office where it is assigned to the appropriate claims representative or service representative.

If you belong to a group or an organization that would like to hear a speaker on Social Security matters, you can call your local district office and ask the field representative to make a speech. Field representatives frequently work at night and on weekends for these purposes. The field representative's broad-based knowledge is usually sufficient to answer all general questions.

Receptionist

When you go to your district office, you will be greeted at the front desk by the *receptionist* who will ask your name and a few questions to determine the nature of your visit. It is his or her job to determine which employee should service you. At the district office, different types of business are handled by different employees.

In addition to the reception duties, the receptionist usually handles matters dealing with Social Security numbers, such as applications for new numbers or changing names for the Social Security records. The receptionist has little training outside those duties and it is not a good idea to take advice on anything else from the receptionist.

SOCIAL SECURITY TIP

Some overzealous receptionists have been known to give erroneous information about Social Security matters. It is wise to take your advice only from a claims or service representative.

After taking your name and determining the nature of your visit, the receptionist will generally ask you to be seated and will assign you to the next available representative who handles your type of case. It is possible that other persons who have arrived after you will be taken care of first because a representative who handles their type of business is available before a representative who handles your type of business.

SECTION 107 THE PROGRAMS OPERATIONS MANUAL SYSTEM

The *Programs Operations Manual System* (POMS) is the rulebook used by all district office personnel. These manuals are issued by the Central Office and provide the working rules and interpretations of the law and regulations. The official regulations of the Social Security Administration, which are published in the

Federal Register and available in law libraries, are almost never used by the personnel in the district offices. Instead, they rely almost exclusively upon the POMS. The POMS is available in every district office for review by members of the public. Generally, the policy of the Social Security office is to require an interviewer to be present while a member of the public reviews the POMS. This is required because much of the language is written in bureaucratic shorthand that can be meaningless to most people. A claims representative or service representative will be required to interpret this bureaucratic language. The POMS is the *bible* of the Social Security Administration and all decisions must be founded upon the provisions contained in these manuals. If you doubt the accuracy of information given to you by any Social Security interviewer, you should ask to see where it is stated in the POMS. The interviewer should be able to locate the pertinent section to show you in black and white.

The POMS is available online through the SSA's website. Go to **http://policy.ssa.gov/poms.nsf/aboutpoms** for further information. Be forewarned—these rules are laced with acronyms and bureaucratic shorthand.

ELIGIBILITY REQUIREMENTS 2

SECTION 201 ELIGIBILITY REQUIREMENTS— IN GENERAL

The Social Security Act provides for the payment of many different types of Social Security benefits. The benefits usually referred to as Social Security benefits are provided under the basic programs known as *Retirement Insurance, Survivors Insurance, Disability Insurance* (RSDI), and *Health Insurance*, better known as Medicare. These benefits are funded by taxes on earnings—the FICA taxes that are deducted from paychecks. There are many other social insurance and welfare programs in the United States, some administered by the

Social Security Administration (SSA) and some administered by the states. (This book only discusses Social Security benefits, although the Supplemental Security Income (SSI) program is briefly discussed in Chapter 14.)

> ***Caution***: Many people confuse SSI with Social Security, because the SSI program provides payments for the aged and the disabled, and both are administered by the SSA. Some Social Security beneficiaries whose benefit amounts are low are eligible to receive additional payments under the SSI program. To really muddle it, all the double-S acronyms confuse even lawyers and accountants, so it is not surprising that most people get mixed up. In a nutshell, Social Security benefits are based on the taxed earnings of workers, and paid to them, their dependents, and their survivors. It is called an *entitlement program* and pays *benefits*. *Supplemental Security Income* (SSI) is a federally administered (by the SSA) welfare program for the elderly, the disabled, and the blind. The SSI program makes *payments* to supplement the income of the needy recipient. If the recipient's income exceeds certain levels, which can vary by state, then SSI payments are suspended. Unlike SSI, Social Security benefits are entitlements, so the beneficiary is paid regardless of income. The exceptions to that are in the cases of earned income that may indicate that a disabled worker is not in fact disabled or a retired worker is not retired. Unearned income, such as pensions, dividends, interest, annuities, etc., do not affect eligibility for Social Security benefits.

There are specific eligibility requirements that a claimant must meet in order to receive each Social Security benefit. Even though a person becomes entitled, a benefit may not be paid for one of several reasons, often because earnings are in excess of the applicable limits. This chapter deals only with the basic eligibility requirements. (see Chapter 8.) Additionally, almost all benefits require an application to be filed by the claimant. (see Chapter 4.)

Each type of benefit requires that the worker on whose record the benefits are based have what is called an *insured status*. This means that he or she has enough work credits. There are different kinds of insured status and some require more work than others. (These different types of insured status will be discussed in detail in Chapter 6. The amount of the actual benefit the beneficiary receives is discussed in detail in Chapter 7.)

Spouses, young children, and disabled adult children of disabled and retired workers are paid monthly benefits if they meet the specific eligibility requirements discussed in this chapter. Surviving widows, widowers, young children, and disabled adult children of deceased workers may also be eligible for benefits.

Benefits are also payable to certain divorced spouses, divorced widow(er)s, and parents of covered workers. There are many different kinds of monthly benefits. Fifteen different types of benefits are categorized in this chapter. Eligibility requirements for each are listed separately. In addition to monthly benefits, the *Social Security Act* also provides for Medicare. This is officially called health insurance and has two parts—*hospital insurance* and *medical insurance*. This is discussed more fully in Chapter 12, while this chapter lists the eligibility requirements.

NOTE: *Eligibility requirements for other programs that are administered by the Social Security Administration, such as Supplemental Security Income (see Sec. 1401) or Black Lung benefits (see Sec. 1402), are not discussed.*

The material explained in Sec. 202 through Sec. 205.4 identifies the various types of benefits one might receive from Social Security. The format by which the material is presented is as follows:

Benefit Name—this is the common reference for the benefit described.

Other Names—this will indicate the other names by which the benefit may be called.

Beneficiary Identification Code—this is a designation used by the SSA for claims. (See Sec. 1407 for more information on the Beneficiary Identification Code and Appendix H for a listing of the code letters.)

Requirements—this details the necessary requirements for the benefit.

Benefit Amount—this states the monthly dollar amount of the benefit before any reductions.

Termination—this identifies when and why the benefit ends. (see Sec. 1009.)

SECTION 202 **RETIREMENT BENEFITS**

Other Names: Old Age Insurance Benefits; Retirement Insurance Benefits.

Beneficiary Identification Code: A

Requirements:

1. You are at least age 62 *throughout the month*. You are not usually eligible until the month after your 62nd birthday. (see Sec. 209.)

2. You have enough work covered by Social Security to be *fully* insured. Generally, this means that you have worked for at least ten years. (see Sec. 602.)

3. You file an application. (See Chapter 4 for a discussion of the filing rules, especially the limits on retroactivity (see Sec. 404.1).)

Benefit Amount: 100% of the *primary insurance amount* (PIA) at *full retirement age*, reduced for any age before full retirement age. Benefits vary greatly, depending on the work record. For 2004, low average earnings may yield a PIA of $721; maximum average earnings can result in a PIA of $1,784. (see Chapter 7.)

NOTE: *Updated information for years after publication is available online at* ***www.socialsecuritybenefitshandbook.com***.

Termination: Entitlement ends with the month before the month of death. (see Sec. 1009.)

SECTION 203 DISABILITY BENEFITS

Other Names: Disability Insurance Benefits; Disabled Worker Benefits.

Beneficiary Identification Code: HA

Requirements:

1. You are under *full retirement age.* (At *full retirement age,* the benefit is converted to an unreduced retirement benefit, even if you are still disabled)

2. You have enough work covered by Social Security to meet the special disability insured status. (see Sec. 604.) Generally, you must have worked at least five years within the preceding ten-year period.

3. You file an application. (See Chapter 4 for a discussion of the filing rules, especially the limits on retroactivity (see Sec. 404.5).)

4. You are totally and permanently disabled for any employment. *Permanent* means that the disability is expected to last at least one year or result in death. (see Sec. 502.)

5. You have been totally disabled for at least five months. (see Sec. 507.)

Benefit Amount: 100% of the primary insurance amount. (See Chapter 7 for a full discussion of computations of benefits.) The disability benefit is not reduced for age but is subject to offset in some cases. (See Secs. 511–512 for the effect of workers' compensation benefits or other disability benefits.)

Termination: Entitlement ends with:

1. The month before you reach *full retirement age.* (You are then automatically switched to retirement benefits.)

2. The second month after the disability ceases. (See Sec. 513 for a discussion of the payment rules at the time of cessation of disability.)

3. The month before the month of death. (See Sec. 1009 for a discussion of the rules about payments at termination.)

SECTION 204 SPOUSE'S BENEFITS

There are several categories of Spouse's Benefits. Each has its own requirements and benefit amounts, which are discussed herein.

Section 204.1 Spouse's Benefits: Age 62 and Older

Other Names: Wife's Benefits; Husband's Benefits; Aged Spouse; Aged Wife; Aged Husband.

Beneficiary Identification Code: B (or HB if the worker received disability benefits)

Requirements:

1. You are the wife or husband of a worker entitled to retirement or disability benefits.

NOTE: *The marriage may be* deemed valid *by the SSA even if it is not legally recognized. (see Sec. 210.)*

2. Your marriage lasted for at least one year. (see Sec. 211.)

3. You are at least age 62 throughout the month. Usually you are not eligible until the month after your 62nd birthday. (see Sec. 209.)

4. You file an application. (See Chapter 4 for a discussion of the filing rules, especially the limits on retroactivity (Sec. 404.4).)

5. You are not entitled to a higher retirement or disability benefit on your own earnings record. (You may be entitled to some spouse's benefits even if you are entitled on your own record, if your benefit is lower than one-half of your spouse's primary insurance amount. (see Sec. 302.)

Benefit Amount: One-half of your spouse's primary insurance amount (see Sec. 702.1) at *full retirement age* reduced for age before *full retirement age* (see Sec. 703) unless you have a child in your care (see Sec. 213); reduced by your own benefit (see Sec. 302); and subject to the family maximum. (see Chapter 7.)

Termination: Entitlement ends with:

1. The month before you become entitled to a higher benefit on your own account. (see Sec. 302.)

2. The month before you become divorced. (You may be able to switch over to divorced spouse's benefit (see Sec. 204.2).)

3. The month before the spouse on whose earnings you receive benefits dies or is no longer disabled. In the event of death, you may switch to a widow(er)'s benefit. (See Sec. 204.4 for requirements and see Sec. 405 for automatic conversion from spouse's to widow(er)'s benefits.)

4. If your benefits are based on a *deemed* marriage (see Sec. 210), the month before you marry someone else or the legal wife of the worker becomes entitled on his account.

5. The month before the month of death. (See Sec. 1009 for a discussion of the rules about payments at termination.)

NOTE: *Spouse's benefits are now gender neutral. You may be eligible either as the husband or the wife of the worker. Whenever the term wife's benefits is used in this book, you may substitute husband's benefits, if applicable.*

Section 204.2 Spouse's Benefits: With Child in Care

Other Names: Young Wife; Young Husband; Young Spouse.

Beneficiary Identification Code: B2 (or HB2 if the worker receives disability benefits)

Requirements: The requirements are the same as an aged spouse (see Sec. 204.1), with one exception—you may collect at any age as long as you have a child of the worker in your care (see Sec. 213) who is entitled to child benefits on the worker's account, and who is either under age 16 or a disabled child of any age for whom you are rendering substantial personal services. (See Secs. 205.1–205.4 for who qualifies as children.)

Benefit Amount: 50% of the spouse's primary insurance amount. (see Sec. 702.) There is no reduction for being under *full retirement age*. The benefit is subject to reduction for the family maximum. (see Chapter 7.)

Termination: Occurs the same as for aged spouse's benefits (see Sec. 204.1) and the month before the month the youngest child turns 16 years old. (see Sec. 213.)

NOTE 1: *Spouse's benefits are gender neutral. You may be entitled whether you are the wife or the husband of the covered worker.*

NOTE 2: *The benefits may be suspended for any month you do not have a child in your care. (see Sec. 213 and Sec. 1008.)*

Section 204.3 Spouse's Benefits: Divorced Spouse

Other Names: Divorced Wife; Divorced Husband.

Beneficiary Identification Code: B6

Requirements:

1. Your ex-spouse (the worker) is entitled to retirement or disability benefits. A divorced spouse may be *independently entitled* if divorced at least two years. This means the divorced spouse may receive benefits even though the worker has not yet filed or if the benefits are being suspended because of excess earnings. The two-year requirement is designed to avoid any incentive for divorce solely to take advantage of this provision. If the ex-spouse has not filed, he or she must be *eligible*, *insured* (see Chapter 6), and either age 62 or disabled.

NOTE: *The worker's earnings will have no effect on the ex-spouse's benefits under the work test if the worker's first month of entitlement is prior to the month the divorce becomes final. If the worker first becomes entitled in or after the month of divorce, then his or her earnings in excess of the work test may affect the ex-spouse's benefit payment, but only for two years.*

2. You are the wife or husband of the worker as defined by the SSA. (see Sec. 210.)

3. You had been married to the worker for at least ten years immediately before the divorce became final. This requirement is met even if this period was interrupted by a prior divorce from the same spouse, provided the remarriage took place in the calendar year of the divorce or the calendar year immediately following. The marriage must be in existence in each of the ten years before the divorce in order for the claimant to be entitled. You may also qualify based on a ten-year marriage immediately before a prior divorce.

4. You file an application. (see Chapter 4.)

5. You are age 62 throughout the month. (see Sec. 209.) You cannot be entitled as a divorced spouse if you are under age 62, even if you do have a child in your care.

6. You are not entitled to a higher retirement or disability benefit on your own account. (see Sec. 302.)

7. You are unmarried.

Benefit Amount: Same as aged spouse (see Sec. 204.1), but not subject to the *family maximum.*

Termination: Entitlement ends with:

1. The same conditions for an aged wife. (see Sec. 204.1.)

2. When you remarry. However, you may continue to be eligible if you remarry certain other Social Security beneficiaries. (see Sec. 904.)

Section 204.4 Spouse's Benefits: Widow(er), Age 60 and Over

Other Names: Widow's Insurance Benefit; Widower's Insurance Benefit; Aged Widow; Aged Widower.

Beneficiary Identification Code: D

Requirements:

1. The worker to whom you were married died fully insured. (see Chapter 6.)

2. You were *married* to the worker. This may include situations other than legal marriages. (see Sec. 210.)

3. You were married for at least nine months before the worker died. (See Sec. 212 for exceptions to this requirement.)

4. You file an application. (See Chapter 4 for a discussion of the filing rules, especially the limits on retroactivity (Sec. 404.5) and for automatic conversion from spouse to widow(er) (Sec. 405).)

5. You are at least age 60.

   NOTE: *The special "throughout the month" rule for retire-ment and spouse benefits discussed in Sec. 209 does not apply to widow(er)'s benefits.*

6. You are not actually entitled to a higher retirement or disability benefit on your own account. (see Sec. 303.)

7. You are not married. (If you remarry after age 60, then you are not married for Social Security purposes.)

NOTE: *Even though a widow(er) could meet all the requirements, entitlement is precluded if: (1) the widow(er) was convicted of the felonious and intentional homicide of the worker or (2) the Railroad Retirement Board has jurisdiction of the survivor's claim.*

Benefit Amount: 100% of the worker's *primary insurance amount* plus delayed retirement credits. The benefit amount is reduced if you take it before *full retirement age,* but cannot be reduced below 71%. The benefit amount cannot exceed the worker's benefit amount paid during his or her life. (see Sec. 703.4.) (See Chapter 3 if you also worked on your own account.)

Termination: Entitlement ends with:

1. The month before you become entitled to a higher retirement or disability benefit on your own account. (See Sec. 303 for a discussion of dual entitlement.)

2. If you are entitled based on a *deemed marriage* (see Sec. 210), benefits will end if another person becomes entitled as the legal widow or widower.

3. The month before the month of death. (see Sec. 1009.)

NOTE: *Widow(er)'s benefits are gender neutral.*

Section 204.5 Spouse's Benefits: Mother/Father with Child in Care

Other Names: Young Widow; Mother's Benefits; Father's Benefits.

Beneficiary Identification Code: E

Requirements:

1. The worker died fully or currently insured. (see Chapter 6.)

2. You were married to the worker. (see Sec. 210.)

3. You file an application. (See Chapter 4, especially Sec. 405.)

4. You are unmarried.

5. You are not entitled to a higher widow's benefits on another account or to a higher retirement or disability benefit on your own account. (see Chapter 3.)

6. You have a child in your care. (see Sec. 213.)

Benefit Amount: 75% of the worker's primary insurance amount (see Sec. 702), subject to the family maximum. (see Sec. 703.6.)

Termination: Entitlement ends with the month before the month in which any of the following occur:

1. You become entitled to a higher benefit on another account.

2. The child in your care turns 16 unless the child is disabled and you are rendering services for that child. (See Sec. 213, the Child in Care Requirement.) If you are entitled because you have a disabled adult child in your care, the benefits will end if the child is no longer disabled.

3. You remarry. (For exceptions if you remarry another Social Security beneficiary, see Sec. 904.)

4. If your entitlement is based on a deemed marriage (see Sec. 210), and another person becomes entitled on the account as the legal widow.

5. The month before the month of death.

NOTE: *If your benefits end because you have remarried, they may be reinstated if the subsequent marriage is terminated. (see Sec. 904.) Benefits are gender neutral.*

Section 204.6 **Spouse's Benefits: Disabled Widow(er)'s Benefits (Age 50 to 59)**

Other Names: Disabled Widow's Insurance Benefit; Disabled Widower's Insurance Benefit.

Beneficiary Identification Code: W

Requirements: The requirements are the same as for an aged widow (see Sec. 204.4), except that instead of being 60, you must meet the following requirements.

1. You are at least age 50.

2. You are totally disabled. (see Sec. 502.)

3. The disability started not later than seven years after the worker's death or seven years after you were last entitled to mother's or father's benefits (see Sec. 204.5) or disabled widow(er)'s benefits, if you were previously entitled.

4. The disability lasts for more than five months (see Sec. 507) and is expected to last at least one year. (see Sec. 502.)

Benefit Amount: 71% of the worker's *primary insurance amount.* (See Sec. 702.) (See Chapter 7 for a full discussion of computations of benefits.)

Termination: Entitlement ends with the same events as the widow (see Sec. 204.4) and when the disability ends. (see Sec. 513.) For the disabled widow, remarriage after age 50 is not considered for Social Security purposes.

NOTE: *Disabled Widow's benefits are gender neutral.*

Section 204.7 Spouse's Benefits: Divorced Widow(er)'s Benefits

Other Names: Surviving Divorced Wife; Surviving Divorced Husband; Divorced Widower; Divorced Mother; Divorced Father.

Beneficiary Identification Code: D6 (divorced aged widow); E1 (divorced young widow—child in care); W6 (disabled divorced widow)

Requirements:

1. The worker died fully insured or in the case of a young widow, currently insured. (See Chapter 6 for a discussion of insured status.)

2. You were legally married.

   NOTE: *The deemed valid marriage discussed in Sec. 210 is not sufficient.*

3. The marriage lasted for at least ten years immediately before the divorce.

4. You file an application. (see Chapter 4.)

5. You are age 60, disabled (see Sec. 502), or have a child of the worker in your care. (see Sec. 213.)

6. You are not entitled to a higher retirement or disabled benefit on your own account. (see Sec. 303.)

7. You are unmarried.

Benefit Amount: Same as for a nondivorced widow, but not subject to the *family maximum.* (see Sec. 703.6.)

Termination: Entitlement ends under the same conditions described in Sec. 204.4 for an aged widow, Sec. 204.6 for a disabled widow, or Sec. 204.5 for a young widow.

Section 205 **Child's Benefits**

Social Security benefits are payable to certain children of retired, deceased, or disabled workers. The most common benefit is for the children under age 18. These benefits can be extended if the child is still in high school through the end of the semester or quarter in which the child turns age 19. No benefits are payable after that, even if the child continues on to college. Benefits for children in college were eliminated many years ago, but benefits are payable to adult children who become disabled before age 22. The grandchildren of covered workers may be eligible for benefits provided that the parents are either deceased or totally disabled at the time the worker became eligible for benefits. The requirements for these benefits are discussed in detail in the following sections.

Section 205.1 **Child's Benefits: Under Age 18**

Other Names: Surviving Child; Dependent Child.

Beneficiary Identification Code: C (HC if the worker receives disability benefits)

Requirements:

1. The worker is entitled to retirement or disability benefits, or in the case of survivors, died either fully insured (see Sec. 602) or currently insured. (see Sec. 603.)

2. You are the child of the worker as defined in Sec. 214. Under certain circumstances this can include stepchildren, illegitimate children, adopted children, and grandchildren.

3. You are dependent on the worker at the time he or she becomes eligible for retirement or disability benefits or dies. (see Sec. 215.) If you are the natural child of the worker, you are deemed dependent.

4. You file an application. (see Chapter 4.)

5. You are unmarried.

6. You are under age 18. (See Sec. 205.2 for students and Sec. 205.3 for disabled adult children.)

Benefit Amount: Children entitled on a living worker's account receive 50% of the primary insurance amount. (see Sec. 702.1.) Children entitled on a deceased worker's account receive 75% of the primary insurance amount. In all cases it is subject to the family maximum. (See Chapter 7 for a full discussion of computations.)

Termination: Entitlement ends with the month before any of the following events occur:

1. You turn 18 years old (if you are a student or disabled, see Sec. 205.2 and Sec. 205.3).

2. You marry.

3. The worker's entitlement ends for a reason other than death. If the worker dies, you will be converted to a survivor benefit as a child.

4. You die.

Section 205.2 **Child's Benefits: High School Student**

Other Names: Full-Time Student.

Beneficiary Identification Code: C

Requirements:

1. The requirements are the same as for a child under age 18, except that you do not have to be under age 18.

2. You must be no older than age 19. Benefits may continue for up to three months after age 19 if you turn age 19 during the school quarter or semester.

3. You must be a full-time student in an approved elementary or secondary school, or an approved home school program. A high school level program taken in a college, community college, vocational school, or technical school qualifies if the program is approved as a secondary level school program by the Board of Education or the state.

4. You must not be paid by your employer to attend school.

Benefit Amount: Same as for a child under 18. (see Sec. 205.1.)

Termination: Entitlement ends with the month before any of the following events occur:

1. You turn 18 years old and are no longer a full-time student.

2. You start to be paid by your employer to attend school.

3. You marry.

4. The worker's entitlement ends for a reason other than death. If the worker dies, you will be converted to a survivor benefit as a child.

5. You die.

NOTE: *A school is considered approved if it is accredited by the state in which it is located and its primary purpose is to provide secondary or elementary education. Full-time means twenty hours per week and at least a thirteen-week course. Home schooling qualifies if the student meets the federal standards for full-time attendance—twenty hours per week for thirteen weeks, and not a correspondence course. The state recognizes home school as an educational institution even after the student turns 16, when some states no longer require compulsory education.*

Section 205.3 Child's Benefits: Disabled Adult Child

Other Names: Childhood Disability Beneficiary; Adult Disabled Child.

Beneficiary Identification Code: C

Requirements:

1. The requirements are the same as Sec. 205.1, except that you must be age 18 or older.

2. You become totally disabled before you reach age 22. (see Sec. 502.)

NOTE: *If your benefits stop when you turn age 18, they may be reestablished if you become disabled before age 22.*

Benefit Amount: Children entitled on a living worker's account receive 50% of the primary insurance amount. (see Sec. 702.1.) Children entitled on a deceased worker's account receive 75% of the primary insurance amount. In all cases, it is subject to the family maximum. (see Chapter 7.)

Termination: Entitlement ends with:

1. Your marriage. (In some cases, marriage to another Social Security beneficiary does not terminate a disabled child's benefits.) (see Sec. 1009.)

2. When the disability ceases. (see Sec. 513.) If you become disabled again after the disability ceases, the benefit may resume if you become disabled for the second time within seven years after the month in which your disabled child benefits ended.

3. The worker's entitlement ends for a reason other than death. If the worker dies, you will be converted to a survivor benefit as a child.

4. Your death.

Section 205.4 **Child's Benefits: Grandchildren**

Other Names: These are referred to as Child's Benefits even though the entitlement is based on a grandchild relationship.

Beneficiary Identification Code: C

Requirements:

Grandchildren may be eligible for benefits if they meet the requirements for children's benefits discussed in the preceding sections in addition to these requirements.

1. You are the child of the covered worker's child. (see Sec. 214.)

2. Your parents were both either deceased or totally disabled (see Sec. 502) at the time the grandparent first became entitled to retirement benefits, disability benefits, or died. If the grandparent died after becoming entitled to benefits, you must have met the requirements as of the date he or she became entitled to benefits.

3. You are dependent on the grandparent. (see Sec. 215.)

Benefit Amount: The benefit amount of grandchildren's benefits is the same as for regular children's benefits.

Termination: The benefits end under the same conditions as those for other types of children's benefits.

SECTION 206 PARENT'S BENEFITS

NOTE: *These benefits are payable only to surviving parents of deceased workers. They are not payable if the worker is alive.*

Other Names: Father, Mother, Stepfather, Stepmother (F1, F2, F3, F4, respectively).

Beneficiary Identification Code: F

Requirements:

1. The worker died fully insured. (see Sec. 602.)

2. You are the natural parent of the worker according to the laws of the state where the worker had a permanent home. If you adopted the worker, you must have adopted him or her before he or she was age 16. If you are a stepparent, you must have married the worker's natural parent before the worker became 16 years old.

3. You are at least age 62.

4. You have not married since the worker died.

5. You file an application. (see Chapter 4.)

6. You are not entitled to a retirement or disability greater than the parent's benefit amount.

7. You received at least one-half of your support from the worker at the time he or she died or became disabled if the disability continued up to the time of death.

NOTE: *Proof of support must be filed with the Social Security Administration within two years of the death of the worker or the date he or she became eligible for benefits. If this proof is not filed within two years of the worker's death or disability, whether or not you are eligible to start receiving benefits at that time, you cannot be eligible at a later date, unless you can establish good cause for not filing it timely. You may also be eligible for an exception provided by the Servicemembers' Civil Relief Act. It would be wise to consult an attorney if the proof of support was not filed within two years of the worker's death or disability.*

Benefit Amount: The amount of the parent's benefit depends on whether there are one or two parents entitled on the account. If there is one eligible parent, the benefit is 82½% of the worker's primary insurance amount. (see Sec. 702.1.) If there are two eligible parents, it is 75% of the worker's primary insurance amount, payable to each parent. It is subject to reduction for the family maximum. (See Chapter 7 for a full discussion of computation of benefits.)

Termination: Ends with entitlement to a higher retirement benefit on your own account, death, or marriage. (See Appendix I for exceptions.)

SECTION 207.1 MEDICARE GENERALLY

This section discusses only the basic eligibility requirements for Medicare. Coverage provisions (what Medicare pays for) are discussed in Chapter 12 and application requirements are discussed in Chapter 4.

Medicare has three parts: Hospital Insurance (Part A), Medical Insurance (Part B), called Original Medicare, and Prescription Drug Coverage (Part D), which is optional for those who are eligible for Medicare, and is provided by private companies. Medicare Advantage Plans, referred to as Part C, are another option available in some areas of the country. The Medicare Advantage plans provide hospital, medical and drug coverage through Health Maintenance Organizations (HMOs), Preferred provider organizations (PPOs) and several other types of arrangements. Hospital Insurance primarily pays for in-patient care and Medical Insurance covers doctor bills. Both parts A and B also cover other charges as well (see Chapter 12). Drug coverage is available through some Medicare Advantage Plans or Part D. There are limits for filing an application for Medicare coverage. If you do not file timely you may lose coverage and have to pay an extra premium for Medical Insurance (Sec. 407), and for Part D Prescription Drug Coverage (Sec. 1203.2). You may enroll in Part D Prescription Drug Coverage if you are eligible for either Part A or Part B. Part D enrollment is made directly to the private company you choose for this coverage. (see Sec. 1203.1.)

Section 207.1 **Hospital Insurance**

There are three groups of individuals eligible for Medicare Hospital Insurance. The first group is those age 65 or older who either:

- Receive of any Social Security monthly benefit or Railroad Retirement Board monthly benefit or are eligible for them. An application must be filed for Medicare even if you are still working. (see Sec. 404.3); or

- Are federal employees with sufficient quarters of coverage (federal employees started having Medicare tax withheld from their paychecks effective January of 1983). There are special provisions to grant credit for those employees for work performed before 1983, if they were employed by the federal government in January 1984; or

- Pay a monthly premium and who are either U.S. citizens or lawfully admitted resident aliens who have resided in the United States for five continuous years or more.

The second group eligible for Hospital Insurance includes those individuals who are entitled to monthly Social Security disability benefits (including disabled adult children and disabled widows) or disabled federal employees with enough work covered for Medicare purposes. The coverage for these groups begins with the twenty-fifth month of disability benefits entitlement, not counting the waiting period. (see Sec. 507.) For those disabled with a primary or secondary diagnosis of Amyotrophic Lateral Sclerosis (ALS)—also called Lou Gerhig's Disease—Medicare coverage begins with the *first* month of disability benefits entitlement.

The third group includes those individuals who suffer from end-stage renal disease (kidney failure) and:

- undergo a regular course of dialysis or have a kidney transplant, and are either fully or currently insured (see Secs. 602 and 603);

- are the spouse or former spouse (married at least ten years) of someone who is fully or currently insured; or,

- if under age twenty-five when kidney failure occurs, are children of a worker who is fully or currently insured.

NOTE: *The spouse or parent of the kidney patient need not be eligible for or collecting Social Security benefits. For example, a wage earner who is age 50 and working full time is not eligible for monthly Social Security benefits, but his or her spouse or children under age 25 can still be entitled to Medicare on the wage earner's record under this provision.*

Section 207.2 **Medical Insurance**

There are three groups of people who are eligible for Medicare medical insurance.

The first group includes people age 65 or over who are U.S. citizens (or legal aliens admitted for permanent residence and who have resided in the country for five continuous years or more) and who pay the monthly premium. You do not have to be eligible for Medicare hospital insurance or any other Social Security benefit to be eligible for medical insurance.

The second group of people is comprised of those eligible for hospital insurance on the basis of disability who pay the monthly premium. (see 207.1.)

The third group includes those entitled to Medicare hospital insurance for the end-stage renal disease and who pay the monthly premium. (see Sec. 207.1.)

SECTION 208 LUMP SUM DEATH PAYMENT

A lump sum in the amount of $255 is payable to certain survivors of a worker who died fully or currently insured. (see Chapter 6.) A benefit is paid to only one person (with the exception of children) according to the following order of priority.

1.   The surviving spouse who was living in the same household with the worker at the time of death.

2. A surviving spouse not living in the same household but potentially entitled to monthly benefits on the deceased worker's account in the month of death.

3. If there are neither of the above, then the payment is made to the surviving children of the worker who are eligible for monthly benefits on the account. All the surviving children split the lump sum death benefit evenly.

Only $255 is paid, even if it is split among the surviving children. If there are no people who fit these categories, there is no lump sum death benefit payable.

The application for this benefit must be filed within two years of the death of the worker.

Section 209 Being Age 62 "Throughout the Month"

Social Security has a special rule that applies to retired workers and their spouses who file for benefits beginning at age 62. You cannot receive a retirement benefit or an aged spouse's benefit unless you are age 62 *throughout the entire month*. Generally, this means that you cannot receive a Social Security benefit for the month of your 62nd birthday, because you are not age 62 throughout that entire month. This rule does not apply to widows.

If your 62nd birthday is on the first day of the month, you will be eligible because you will be age 62 throughout the month. If your birthday is on the second day of the month, then you are eligible for that month as well, because for Social Security purposes you attain your age the day before your birthday.

Example: If you were born on August 2, you become age 62 on August 1 for Social Security purposes. Therefore, you are eligible to receive the benefit for that month. If your birthday was on August 3, your first month of eligibility would be September.

You can be eligible for benefits for any month after the month you turn 62 years old.

Section 210 Marriage Requirement

In order to qualify for spouse's benefits or for widow(er)'s benefits, the claimant must have been married to the worker. Generally, this means that the marriage must be recognized as valid in the state where it was performed. A common-law marriage will be accepted by Social Security only if entered into in a state that recognizes common-law marriages. Most states do not.

A person may meet the marriage requirement even if he or she was not legally married to the worker, if the following five conditions are met.

1. There was a marriage ceremony.

2. The claimant married the worker in good faith not knowing any impediment to the marriage.

3. The claimant was living with the worker at the time of his or her entitlement to benefits or at the time of death.

4. There is no other person entitled on the worker's earnings record as a legal wife or widow.

5. There was a legal impediment or there was a defect in the procedure followed in connection with the marriage ceremony. A legal impediment exists, for example, when the worker was already married at the time of this marriage.

This provision is called the *deemed valid* marriage. If your benefits are based on a deemed valid marriage, they will end if another person becomes entitled on the account as the legal wife or widow. You may be reentitled when that other person's entitlement ends.

SECTION 211 EXCEPTIONS TO THE ONE-YEAR DURATION OF MARRIAGE REQUIREMENT FOR SPOUSE'S BENEFITS

In most cases, to be eligible as the spouse of a worker, the marriage must have lasted for a least one year before eligibility begins. However, there are some exceptions to this general rule. These exceptions are as follows.

- The claimant is the natural parent of the worker's child. This requirement is met if a live child was born to the worker and the claimant even though the child may not be alive at the time the claimant applies for benefits.

- The claimant was entitled or potentially entitled (under Social Security or Railroad Retirement) to spouse's benefits, widow's benefits, parent's benefits, or childhood disability benefits in the month before the month of marriage to the worker. *Potentially entitled* means that you could have received benefits if you had applied for them. Your age is not considered when determining whether or not you are potentially entitled.

SECTION 212 EXCEPTIONS TO THE NINE-MONTH DURATION OF MARRIAGE REQUIREMENT FOR WIDOW(ER)'S BENEFITS

The general rule is that to be eligible for widow's benefits, you must have been married to the worker for at least nine months before the death of the worker. There are some exceptions to this rule. The exceptions that apply to spouses (see Sec. 211) also apply to widow(er)s, in addition to the following.

- The worker died because of an accident.

- The worker's death occurred in the line of duty while he or she was a member of a uniformed service on active duty.

- The claimant was previously married to the worker and divorced from him or her, and the previous marriage lasted at least nine months.

NOTE: *For these three exceptions to apply, the worker must have been expected to live for at least nine months at the time of marriage.*

SECTION 213 CHILD IN CARE REQUIREMENT

If you are the spouse or widow(er) of a covered worker, you may be eligible for benefits at any age if you have a child of the worker in your care. To meet this requirement, the child must be entitled on the same earnings record as the one on which you are making your claim. The child must be under age 16 or disabled. If the child is disabled and over 16, you can be eligible if you are performing personal services for the disabled child. *Personal services* include such things as helping the child wash him- or herself, feeding the child, dressing the child, and so forth. Personal services require that you render more services than for a nondisabled child.

NOTE: *The child may continue to receive benefits until age 18, but your entitlement will end when the child turns 16 years old unless he or she is disabled.*

The child does not have to be physically in your custody to meet the *in care* requirement. If you are exercising parental control and responsibility over the upbringing of the child, you may still satisfy the requirement.

Example: If the child is away at boarding school, you may still be eligible if you are reviewing his or her work and providing parental guidance.

If you are separated from the other parent of the child, you cannot meet the *child in care* requirement while the child is in the custody of the other parent. A child is considered in your care if he or she is with you at least one day of the month.

Example: If the child goes to the other parent on July 15 and comes back to you on August 15, you will meet the requirement for both July and August. However if the child did not come back until September 15, you would not meet the requirement for the month of August.

For any month in which the child is not in your care, you are not entitled to benefits and they are suspended. Once the child returns to your care, the benefits may resume.

SECTION 214 CHILD RELATIONSHIP REQUIREMENT

In addition to a *natural child*, certain other kinds of children can be eligible for Social Security benefits. These are adoptive children, stepchildren, equitably adopted children, and grandchildren.

To be eligible, an *adopted child* must either have been adopted before the worker becomes eligible for benefits or before the child becomes age 18. If the child turned 18 years old and was adopted after the worker becomes entitled, then the child must have received one-half support from the worker and lived with him or her for the twelve-month period preceding the worker's entitlement to benefits. The adoption must be legal.

The *stepchild* must be dependent on the worker (see Sec. 215) and the marriage of the stepchild's parent to the worker must have lasted one year (nine months for survivor cases). If the stepchild is entitled, the benefits will not be terminated even if the parents divorce at a later date.

A child may be *equitably adopted* if there was an intent by the worker to adopt the child but the worker was unable to complete the legal requirements. If you have a possible case involving equitable adoption, you should consult an attorney.

Grandchildren may be eligible on the grandparents' account, but only if all of the requirements described in Sec. 205.4 are met. Generally, this means that the parents are either deceased or totally disabled at the time the worker (the grandparent) becomes entitled to benefits, becomes disabled, or dies, whichever is earliest.

Section 215 Dependency Requirements— Children and Grandchildren

The natural and adoptive children of a worker are deemed dependent upon him or her. This means that there is no requirement for proof of dependency. However, in all other cases, there must be proof that the child was dependent on the worker for at least one-half of his or her support in the year before the worker became eligible for benefits or died (in survivor cases).

Basically, Social Security will itemize all the reasonable and necessary expenses for the child's food, clothing, shelter, and education, and will total these expenses. If the worker was making contributions to the child's support equal to or greater than one-half of these living expenses, the dependency requirement will be met.

ENTITLEMENT ON MORE THAN ONE ACCOUNT **3**

SECTION 301 ENTITLEMENT ON MORE THAN ONE ACCOUNT—IN GENERAL

Under certain circumstances, you may be entitled to benefits based upon two or more separate Social Security accounts. This chapter explains these situations.

NOTE: *Throughout this chapter, reference is made to full retire-ment age. Beginning with those born in 1938 (for retirement and spouse benefits) and 1940 (for widow(er)'s benefits), the age at which unreduced benefits are paid has increased. In the past, benefits were reduced if taken before full retirement age. This age limit is going up in increments. The increase in full retirement age depends on the year of birth. (see Sec. 703.)*

SECTION 302 ON YOUR OWN EARNINGS RECORD AND AS A HUSBAND/WIFE

The general rules are as follows.

- You must file on your own account if you have enough quarters of coverage to be fully insured. (see Sec. 602.)

- You must file on your spouse's account as a wife or husband if your spouse is then entitled to benefits and your *primary insurance amount* is less than one-half of his or hers.

The second rule applies if your husband or wife has applied and become entitled, even if not actually receiving monthly benefits because they are being suspended (usually due to earnings). If your spouse is not entitled because he or she has not yet applied, this rule does not operate because you cannot be eligible on an account that has not yet been established.

A person who is entitled to a retirement or disability benefit and to a spouse's benefit will receive his or her own benefit, reduced for age if the retirement benefit is taken before full retirement age, plus the difference between one-half of the spouse's primary insurance amount and his or her own. The difference will be reduced for age if taken before full retirement age, with the spouse's reduction factor for age figured as of the time of entitlement to the spouse's benefit.

Example: Howard and Wanda are husband and wife. They are both the same age, have both worked, and are each eligible for retirement benefits. Howard is working full time with substantial earnings. Wanda is not working. They are both age 62. Wanda applies for her retirement benefit. Her primary insurance amount is $800. Because she is under full retirement age, her benefit is reduced to $640. Two years later, Howard retires and files for retirement benefits. His primary insurance amount is $1,800. Wanda decides to apply for wife's benefits on his account. She has the option of waiting until she has reached full retirement age to file for the wife's benefit, because when she applied for her retirement benefit on her own account, her husband was not entitled since he had not applied.

The amount of her wife's benefit is derived by taking one-half of her husband's primary insurance amount ($1,800 divided by 2 = $900), subtracting her primary insurance amount ($800) and then reducing the difference ($100) by the number of months before full retirement age at that time, which in this example is 12. Using the wife's reduction factor (see Sec. 703.2), the $100 difference is reduced to $91. In this case then, Wanda receives $640 on her own account plus $91 on her husband's account as a wife.

The second rule can result in an unwanted reduction of a spouse's benefit.

Example: When the husband is working, but is *entitled* to a retirement benefit that is not being paid because of the excess earnings (this can happen, for example, if there is a change in retirement plans), the wife's benefit amount is figured at the age she becomes entitled, even though she may not receive benefits due to work deductions caused by the husband's earnings. If she is under full retirement age, that reduction rate will apply to any benefits she may eventually receive when the husband's work deductions cease and the wife's benefit is paid.

As with Howard and Wanda, if Howard had applied before or with Wanda, then Wanda's benefit on Howard's account at age 62 would have been approximately $75. If Howard's earnings were too high, the benefit would be withheld due to work deductions, but the benefit amount would stay the same. When Wanda would begin getting the spouse benefit at age 64, and Howard's earnings no longer caused work deductions, Wanda's benefit amount would be $75, not the $91 she would get in the previous example. Fortunately, the reduction factor will be readjusted when Wanda becomes of full retirement age to eliminate months for which benefits were suspended. However, until full retirement age, she will suffer the full reduction.

SECTION 303 ON YOUR OWN ACCOUNT AND WIDOW(ER)'S BENEFITS

If you are potentially eligible on your own earnings record and on the record of your deceased husband or wife, you have different options. Unlike the spouse benefit, you may choose to receive reduced benefits on one account and wait until full retirement age to switch over to unreduced benefits on the other account. The rules that apply to these situations are best discussed according to age.

Under Age 62

Beginning at age 60, you can receive regular widow's benefits reduced for age. If you were born after 1928, the receipt of reduced widow's benefits will have no effect on retirement benefits on your own account if you later switch. You cannot receive retirement benefits on your own account until you attain age 62.

Example: Jane Doe becomes age 60 and applies for widow's benefits. Her husband's primary insurance amount (see Sec. 702.1) is $1,000. The widow's age reduction factor (see Sec. 703) causes a reduction of $285, bringing the monthly payment down to $715, based on sixty reduction months because Jane is sixty months under full retirement age. Jane has also worked and earned enough to be entitled to a retirement benefit on her own account. She continues to receive the widow's benefit until she turns full retirement age and applies for benefits on

her own account. She then can receive an unreduced benefit on her own account, but the widow's
benefit will stop. If the widow's reduced benefit is
higher than her own benefit, she will continue to
receive the widow's benefit amount.

NOTE: *If you were born in 1928 or earlier and you took a
widow's benefit before age 62, it causes a permanent reduction in
your own retirement benefit. The dollar amount of reduction of the
widow's benefit is deducted from your retirement benefit even if
you did not receive the retirement benefit until full retirement age.
However, if the regular age reduction for taking the retirement
benefit before full retirement age is greater, only the greater reduction is used, not both. (see Chapter 8.)*

Between Age 62 and Full Retirement Age

At age 62 you may choose either to take a retirement benefit
on your own account or a widow(er)'s benefit on your
spouse's account. Whichever one you take, it will be reduced
for age by the number of months you are under full retirement
age when you become eligible. (see Sec. 703.) You can take a
reduced benefit on one account before full retirement age and
then switch to the other one unreduced at full retirement age.
Your decision as to which one to take now and which one to
take at full retirement age should be based on the dollar
amount of each benefit, reduced and unreduced.

Before making any decision you must obtain benefit estimates. (see Sec. 1403.) When you contact the Social Security
Administration, make sure that you file a *protective filing*

statement. (see Sec. 402.) When you visit or call your local office, you should deal only with a claims representative to discuss this decision, not a service representative. (see Sec. 106.) It is important to provide the claims representative with recent earnings information to obtain the most accurate estimates. (see Sec. 1403.) The ultimate decision is yours. Social Security cannot suggest which decision you should make, but can give you the information to help you make an educated choice.

Example: Jane Doe retires at age 62. She has worked under Social Security and is a widow. She goes to her district office and learns that her primary insurance amount is $1,000 and that her deceased husband's primary insurance amount is $1,200. Her benefit reduced for age at 62 would be $800 and her widow's benefit reduced for age at 62 would be $994. (see Sec. 703.) She can receive either $800 per month on her own at 62 and then get $1,200 per month on her husband's at full retirement age or she can receive the $994 per month widow's benefit now and then $1,000 per month on her own account at full retirement age.

What should she do?

A helpful way to analyze the situation follows. Jane can receive an extra $194 per month for the thirty-six months she will receive benefits before full retirement age if she takes the widow's benefit first, but she will get $200 less per month starting at full retirement age. If she does this she will receive a total of $6,984 more ($194 x 36 months) before full retirement age. If she does not take this money now and instead decides to wait to get the extra $200 per month, it will take her thirty-five months to get back the benefits she could have received before full retirement age. This analysis does not take into account interest the extra money now could be earning, assuming it was invested.

Not counting interest, if Jane should take the widow's benefit at age 62 instead of her own benefit, she will start losing money approximately three years after she reaches full retirement age. If she took the lower benefits on her own account at age 62, it would take her approximately three years after full retirement age to get back the money she passed up, but after that she would be ahead $200 per month. If her income requirements allow and if she expects a normal life span, it may very well be to Jane's advantage to take the lower benefit on her own account at age 62 and the higher widow's benefit at full retirement age. Of course, if she were on a tight budget or did not expect to live past age 68, she might be better off taking the higher benefit now.

Full Retirement Age and Older

If you are full retirement age or older at the time you first become eligible for benefits, you will receive benefits on the account that has the higher benefit amount. (see Chapter 7.)

SECTION 304 AS A SPOUSE AND AS A WIDOW(ER)

If you are a widow(er) and have remarried, you may be eligible either as a widow(er) or as a spouse. Generally, a widow(er) who remarries cannot collect benefits on a deceased spouse's record, unless he or she has remarried at age 60 or later (age 50 for disabled widows). If you have remarried after you turn age 60 and your spouse is eligible for retirement or disability benefits, you can receive benefits on whichever account gives you the higher benefit. Usually this is the widow(er)'s benefit because the spouse's benefit is only one-half of the worker's *primary insurance amount.* (see Sec. 702.1.) Your entitlement as a widow(er), if you were receiving those benefits before you remarried or before your husband became eligible, will terminate upon your entitlement as a spouse.

SECTION 305 AS A SPOUSE AND AS AN EX-SPOUSE

If you are divorced from a person receiving retirement or disability benefits, you cannot receive benefits as an ex-spouse if you have remarried. In these cases, you can only receive benefits as the spouse of your present husband or wife if he or she is eligible for retirement or disability benefits. You must be married to your new spouse for at least one year before you can be eligible, unless you meet one of the exceptions listed in Section 211.

Section 306 As the Widow(er) of Two or More Workers

If you are the widow(er) of two or more workers, you can receive benefits on the account that gives you the highest benefit. You cannot take one reduced widow(er)'s benefit before full retirement age and then switch to an unreduced widow(er)'s benefit on another account at full retirement age. Once you have picked which account to take widow(er)'s benefits on, you cannot later change to a different worker's account.

Section 307 Disability Benefits and Retirement Benefits

When a person who is under full retirement age is entitled to retirement benefits and is also eligible for disability benefits, he or she has the choice of taking one or the other of these benefits. If you are full retirement age or over, you can take only the retirement benefit. This is equal to the disability benefit. But if you are under full retirement age, the retirement benefit is reduced for age. (see Sec. 703.) The disability benefit is not reduced for age, and so it is usually to your advantage to take the disability benefit. However, if you have two or more eligible dependents, retirement benefits may be better because the *retirement family maximum* may be higher than the *disability family maximum*. (see Sec. 703.6.)

There is a waiting period during which no disability benefits are payable. This period is the first five full months of total disability. (see Sec. 507.) If you are age 62 or older during one or more of the months of the disability waiting period, you can receive the reduced retirement benefit during that time. The retirement benefit will be reduced in the normal fashion depending on your age. (see Sec. 703.) When your disability waiting period is over, you will then switch over to the disability benefit. The disability benefit will be permanently reduced, but only by the number of months you received retirement benefits before switching to disability, not by the full amount of the reduction used to figure the retirement benefit. If you die during the waiting period, widow(er)'s benefits will be permanently reduced by the amount of the retirement age reduction.

Example: John Doe becomes totally disabled beginning with the month he becomes age 62. No disability benefits are payable for the first five months, so he takes reduced retirement benefits starting with age 62. His retirement benefit is reduced by thirty-six months, because he is thirty-six months under full retirement age. When his disability waiting period is up, he switches over to disability benefits. Because he received retirement benefits for only five months before becoming entitled to the disability benefits, his disability benefit is reduced by only five months.

SECTION 308 **CHILD ENTITLED ON MORE THAN ONE ACCOUNT**

A child under age 18 or disabled before age 22 may be entitled on more than one parent's, stepparent's, or grandparent's account. In this case, the child will be paid on the account that gives the highest benefit.

As discussed in Section 703.6, when two or more dependents are entitled on one account, the *family maximum* can limit the total amount of benefits payable so that each dependent may suffer a reduction of the benefit amount payable to him or her. However, when a child is entitled on more than one account and there are other children entitled on one or more of these accounts, the family maximum for each account can be combined so that the reduction of benefits that would otherwise apply can be avoided and each child can receive the full amount payable.

SECTION 309 **OTHER COMBINATIONS OF BENEFITS**

When a beneficiary is entitled to a combination of different benefits other than what has been discussed in the foregoing sections, the basic rule is that he or she will receive the benefit that gives the highest monthly amount. If the beneficiary has worked long enough under Social Security to be entitled to a benefit on his or her own account, then a benefit on that account will be paid, even if it is lower, but the difference will be added from the other account.

APPLICATIONS 4

SECTION 401 APPLICATIONS—IN GENERAL

To be eligible for Social Security monthly benefits or Medicare, an application must be filed with the Social Security Administration (SSA). The SSA has its own forms that must be used for applying for the different kinds of benefits. It is the policy of most SSA offices not to mail out blank application forms, although they will mail forms to an attorney. They prefer their own personnel to complete the applications. This does not necessarily mean that you have to make a personal visit to a district office to file an application. Telephone service is available to file claims. (see Sec. 103.) To do that, you will have to give all the information over the phone to a Social Security employee, who will fill out the

●

application and then mail it to you for your review and signature. Additionally, you may file certain applications, including retirement and disability, over the Internet.

NOTE: *The full retirement age is the age at which you may receive an unreduced benefit. Full retirement age goes up on a gradually increasing basis. (See Sec. 703 for a full discussion.)*

The date the application is filed can be very important. It can affect how much you can receive in past-due benefits. You can protect your filing date before filing a formal application by using a *protective filing statement*. (see Sec. 402.)

Generally, if you believe that you are entitled to benefits, you should file an application. This will require the SSA to make a formal decision on your claim. It will protect your rights to any other benefits you may be entitled to and it will give you the right to appeal if you are dissatisfied.

SOCIAL SECURITY TIP

Occasionally, a person is told (even sometimes by Social Security people) that he or she cannot file an application because he or she does not meet some requirement. This is not true — you can always file an application. If you do not meet the requirements, the application may be denied, but that does not mean that you cannot file it. If there is any doubt, you should file the application to get a formal decision.

SECTION 402 **PROTECTIVE FILING STATEMENT**

A written statement showing an intent to claim benefits filed with the Social Security Administration can protect the filing date for an applicant who files the formal application later. In certain cases, this can prevent a loss of benefits that would otherwise be payable.

As discussed in Sec. 406.1, an application for retirement benefits may not be retroactive in certain cases. This means you cannot receive benefits for any month before the month you file the application, even if you were eligible. But if a protective filing statement is filed, it will protect the filing date of an application filed at a later date. This will allow the payment of retroactive benefits.

Example: John Smith is age 62 in January but is still working. He files a protective filing statement with his local district office in January. In March, he is laid off and will have earnings less than the annual earnings limitation (see Sec. 802.1) so that benefits could be payable starting from January on. If he goes to his local district office in April and files an application for retirement benefits, he can receive past-due benefits starting with January, because he filed a protective filing statement in that month.

If John Smith did not file a protective filing statement, when he goes to the Social Security office in April to file an application for benefits, he can only receive benefits starting in April and continuing from that point. He will lose the benefits for the months of January, February, and March. (see Sec. 406.1.)

In order to qualify as a protective filing statement, the statement must be written; it must indicate an intent to claim benefits; and it must be signed by the claimant, the claimant's spouse, or by a person who could sign an application. (see Sec. 403.) The protective filing statement must be filed with the SSA and will protect benefits starting with the month in which it is filed. A written record made by a Social Security employee of an oral request by a potential claimant can also serve as a protective filing, but it is difficult to prove if the record is lost, which can sometimes happen.

The SSA considers the protective filing statement filed as of the date it receives it or the date it is postmarked by the U.S. Postal Service. In that case, the postmark will be used as the date of filing if that is before it is received by the Social Security Administration.

SOCIAL SECURITY TIP

It is a good idea to mail a protective filing statement by certified or registered mail, return receipt requested, so that you can prove the date it was mailed.

If the postmark is illegible, the SSA presumes it was mailed five days before it is received, unless there is reason to believe that it was mailed later. For example, if the statement is dated only three days earlier than receipt, it will be presumed mailed three days earlier, not five.

The SSA will also accept as a date of filing the date a statement is filed with a Medicare-participating hospital in which you are a patient, as long as the hospital sends the statement to the SSA.

After receiving a protective filing statement, the SSA will send a notice to the claimant advising that an application must be filed within six months. The protective filing statement will be effective for that six-month period. However the six-month period does not begin until Social Security actually sends the notice. If they never do, then the protective filing statement could be good forever.

If you are eligible to receive benefits and you visit your Social Security office to obtain information about benefits, you should file a protective filing statement even if you do not intend to claim benefits immediately. If it turns out a few months later that you could have been eligible when you visited the Social Security office, the protective filing statement could mean additional benefits payable to you.

When filing a protective filing statement, it is a good idea to get a copy. If you visit your district office and the claims representative prepares a written statement for you to sign to protect your filing, ask for a copy and ask that it be date-stamped so that you can prove that it was filed on that date. Protective filing statements have been known to get lost in the local district office. As long as you have your copy with a date stamp, you will not have to worry about that.

There is no set format for the protective filing statement, but it should contain language similar to:

I wish to claim Social Security benefits.

The statement should be signed by the claimant, by the claimant's spouse, or by a person who would be able to file an application. (see Sec. 403.)

SECTION 403 WHO MAY FILE AN APPLICATION

The person who claims benefits must sign an application if he or she is 18 years old or over, is mentally competent, and is physically able to sign. An application for child's benefits may be signed by a parent or a person standing in the place of a parent. A child between the ages of 16 and 18 may sign his or her own application if he or she is mentally competent, has no court-appointed representative, and is not in the care of any person.

If the claimant is a minor, is mentally incompetent, or is physically unable to sign, an application may be signed by a court-appointed representative or a person who is responsible for the care of the claimant, including a relative. If the claimant is in the care of an institution, the manager of the institution may sign the application. The Social Security Administration has the discretion to accept an application signed by someone other than a claimant if it is necessary to protect the claimant from losing benefits.

Example: Mr. Jones becomes bedridden at the end of a month due to a severe medical condition. He asks his neighbor Mr. Smith to go to the Social Security office to file an application for him before the end of the month so that he may receive the benefits for that month. The SSA may accept an application signed by Mr. Smith. However, it would be a good idea if Mr. Jones signed a written statement saying, "I wish to claim Social Security benefits" and gave that statement to Mr. Smith to take to the Social Security office. There would be no doubt that such a statement would be a protective filing statement and could protect that month's benefits. (see Sec. 402.)

Although persons other than the claimant may file an application under certain conditions, the claimant must be alive when the application is filed in order for it to be effective. There are some exceptions to this general rule.

If a disabled person dies before filing an application for disability benefits, a person who would be eligible to receive benefits due to a deceased beneficiary may file the application. (see Sec. 1408.) Although an application for disability benefits may be filed after the worker dies, such an application must be filed within three months after the month of death.

Example: John Smith dies in June. He had been totally disabled for two years before his death but never filed for Social Security benefits. He was married and his wife was living with him. She may file an application for the past-due disability benefits as long as she makes the application or files a protective filing statement no later than September, the third month after his death.

The second exception to the rule is if a protective filing statement was filed by the claimant and he or she died before an application was filed. In such a case, the date of filing is established by the date of the protective filing statement submitted by the claimant, and an application may be filed by a person who would be eligible to receive benefits on the deceased's earnings record or by a person acting for the deceased's estate.

SECTION 404 WHEN TO FILE AN APPLICATION— IN GENERAL

An application may be filed no more than four months before the first month of entitlement. It will be effective until acted upon, but no benefits will be payable until the first actual month of eligibility.

As noted in Sections 406.1 through 407, there are different retroactivity rules for different kinds of applications. If an application is filed after the first month in which you are eligible for benefits, the application may or may not have retroactive effect to entitle you to past-due benefits. The application should be filed before the retroactive life of the application expires so that you do not lose benefits.

Example: In the case of a person who is of full retirement age, an application can be retroactive for up to six months. (see Sec. 406.1.) If you reach full retirement age in March and have no earnings for March or later, you will be eligible for benefits. In order to receive the maximum benefits, you must file the application no later than September. If the application is not filed until October, it can go retroactive for only six months so that the earliest month benefits could begin would be April, and you would lose the benefits for March.

As noted in Section 407, it may be important to file an application before the month you reach age 65, even if you do not intend to collect monthly benefits, to avoid losing some Medicare coverage.

Section 404.1 **When to File for Retirement Benefits**

The rule of thumb frequently heard is that you should file an application for retirement benefits three months before you plan to retire. This is good general advice. However, there are certain situations in which you can actually lose benefits by following this guideline. The *earnings test* (see Sec. 801) and *retroactivity rules* (see Sec. 406.1) work together in such a way that hundreds or even thousands of dollars may be lost if you do not plan in advance.

Depending on the amount of your annual earnings and the amount of your benefit, it is possible to receive some benefits even if you have not retired. An application (or a protective filing statement) must be filed at the right time.

Example: John Smith will reach full retirement age in December of 2007, will work throughout the whole year of 2007, and will earn total annual earnings of $80,000. He goes to the Social Security office to file his application in September. He learns that his unreduced benefit at full retirement age will be $2,100. The benefit figured for January (an eleven-month reduction for age (see Sec. 703)) would be $1,971. Based on his annual earnings, the sum of $15,187 will have to be withheld from any benefits payable to him in 2007. (see Sec. 802.2.) If his month of entitlement to benefits began with January, a total amount of $23,652 ($1,971 x 12) would otherwise be payable for the year, but only the amount of $15,187 would have to be withheld based on his annual earnings, leaving the sum of $8,465 payable.

However, since he did not file his application until September, he will lose these benefits, because an application for retirement benefits cannot be retroactive for months before full retirement age. Although the benefit is reduced for age in determining benefits for January through November, starting with the month of full retirement age it will be readjusted (see Sec. 704.3) to exclude any reduction factor for the months under full retirement age that were withheld to satisfy the earnings test.

Another situation where benefits may be lost, even though you file three months before you retire, is if your countable earnings will be less than the annual earnings limitations. (see Sec. 801.)

Example: Jane Smith will reach full retirement age in May 2007. Her earnings for January through April will be less than $34,440, the yearly limit for those attaining full retirement age in 2007. (Only earnings for months before the month of full retirement age are counted for the earnings limits.) She goes to her local Social Security office in February, three months before May, and files an application for retirement benefits. She will be entitled to monthly benefits beginning with the month of February, the month she filed her application. Because her countable earnings will be less than the annual earnings limitation, she is potentially eligible for benefits for all months of the year she reaches full retirement age.

However, because payment of the benefit for the month of January would result in a permanent reduction for age, her application cannot be retroactive. (see Sec. 406.1.) If she had filed her application in January, she would have been able to receive a benefit for that month. Although this would cause an extra reduction because of age, the reduction would be only a few dollars per month. She could have received hundreds of dollars (or more) for the January benefit.

It is impossible to know whether or not you should file an application for benefits before the usual three-month rule of thumb without knowing the exact benefit amount and the exact amount of your yearly earnings. At the same time, you can request a *benefit estimate* (see Sec. 1403) and then make an informed decision as to when you should start your *retirement benefits*. (see Sec. 408.)

SOCIAL SECURITY TIP

If you will earn less than the annual earnings limit (see Sec. 801) in any year you are at least age 62, you should file a protective filing statement (see Sec. 402) during the month of January of that year.

If you will be working during the year you reach full retirement age, it is a good idea to file a protective filing statement in January even if you do not plan to retire. Request a benefit estimate at the same time. Remember, only earnings for months before you reach full retirement age are counted for the annual earnings test in that year. This way, if it turns out that you can receive benefits by having a January *month of election*, you will be protected. (see Sec. 408.)

If you will have a *nonservice* month (see Sec. 804) at any time after age 62, you should file a protective filing statement no later than the first such month. This is a month when your wages are below the monthly limit, and you do not perform substantial services in self-employment. You may be eligible for a benefit for such a month, despite your annual earnings. In some cases you may not wish to take this benefit, but if you file the protective filing statement, you will preserve your option.

Section 404.2 When to File for Medicare

Medicare has three parts—*hospital insurance, medical insurance*, and *prescription drug coverage*. (see Sec. 1202 and Sec. 1203.1.) An application for hospital insurance may be retroactive for six months. However, unless you will be covered under your employer's group health plan, you must file for medical insurance and drug coverage before the month you turn age 65 to avoid losing some coverage. (see Sec. 407.) Therefore, you should file for Medicare at least one month before you turn age 65, even if you are still working.

NOTE: *Even though full retirement age for monthly benefits has increased, Medicare entitlement still begins at age 65. (see Sec. 703.1.)*

NOTE: *You must enroll in Part D directly with the drug plan you choose, not through Social Security. (see Sec. 1203.2.)*

You have the option of filing only for Medicare, without having to file for retirement benefits. The Social Security Administration prefers you to file the retirement application even if you are working and place your benefits in suspense. This usually makes no difference, but in some cases it does.

If your spouse is under full retirement age and may be eligible for benefits on his or her own account as well as yours, he or she may be better off if you file only the Medicare application if you cannot receive benefits. If your spouse's benefit is less than one-half of yours, he or she will be required to file for spouse's benefits when he or she files for his or her own bene-fits if you are *entitled* on your retirement account, even if you are in work suspense. If he or she is under full retirement age, the amount of your spouse's benefit will be reduced based on his or her age at that time. If you retire before your spouse reaches full retirement age, the extra age reduction for his or her spouse's benefit stays in effect until he or she reaches full retirement age. (see Sec. 302.)

If you are self-employed, you may be able to exclude some of your income from earnings for purposes of the earnings limitation, but you may require a different month of entitlement for retirement. (see Sec. 808.)

If you have a *nonservice* month (see Sec. 804) in the year you turn age 65, but do not wish to use it because you will have more nonservice months in a later year, you may have to restrict your filing to Medicare only. (see Sec. 408.)

SOCIAL SECURITY TIP

Social Security does not usually suggest that you split your entitlement to Medicare from benefits entitlement. It is up to you to specifically request this if it is to your advantage.

Section 404.3 When to File for Survivor's Benefits

As noted in Chapter 2, certain widows, widowers, children, and parents of deceased workers may be eligible for monthly benefits. The earliest such an application can be filed is the month of death of the covered worker. In the case of child's benefits, mothers' or fathers' benefits (these are benefits payable to widows or widowers who have children under 16 or disabled adult children in their care), and in the case of parents' benefits, there is no reduction for age. Therefore, an application for these types of benefits may be retroactive up to six months. (see Sec. 406.1.) Applications for these types of benefits usually should be filed within six months of the date of death.

An application can be filed at a later date so long as the eligibility requirements are still met, but such an application can be retroactive for only six months and benefits may be lost if filed later than six months after the death. Sometimes, however, you may wish to start entitlement at a later date. (see Sec. 408.)

In the case of a disabled widow or widower between the ages of 50 and 59, an application can be retroactive for up to twelve months. (see Sec. 406.1.) If you became disabled after your husband or wife died, you must file an application no later than seventeen months after the beginning of your disability to avoid a loss of any benefits. This is because there is a five-month waiting period before any benefits are payable. (see Sec. 507.) If you became disabled before your husband or wife died, then you must file an application within twelve months of the month of death in order to avoid the loss of any possible monthly benefits. This is because the waiting period during which no benefits are payable may be used up during months before the death of your husband or wife.

In the case of benefits payable to widows or widowers age 60 and over, an application cannot be retroactive if it would result in a payment of a full monthly benefit reduced for age. (see Sec. 406.1.) This means that if you file an application for widow's benefits before you have reached full retirement age, you cannot receive full benefits for any month before the month of filing. (The only exception to this rule is the widow who files for benefits the month after her husband dies. Her application can be retroactive one month *before* the month of death.) Depending on the amount of your earnings and the amount of the benefit, some benefits may be payable even though you are working. (see Sec. 408.) Therefore, it is a good idea to at least file a protective filing statement in the first month in which you may be eligible for widow's or widower's benefits and then obtain benefit estimates to determine whether or not you should file an application. The same principles noted in Section 408 also apply to a widow's claim. You may lose benefits in certain cases if you wait to file until three months before you plan to retire.

If you have worked on your own account and may be eligible for a retirement benefit in addition to the widow's benefit, you will have an option as to which one to receive. (see Sec. 303.) If you are a widow(er) but were entitled to spouse's benefits before your husband or wife died, you may not have to file an application. (see Sec. 405.)

Section 404.4 **When to File for Spouse's and Child's Benefits**

Generally, you should file an application for spouse's and child's benefits at the same time as the worker files. Child's Benefits (see Secs. 205.1–205.4) and Spouse's Benefits—with Child in Care (see Sec. 204.2) are not reduced for age, so usually there is no disadvantage to early filing. These applications may be retroactive for up to six months if the worker is retired. (see Sec. 406.2.) Applications filed after these periods may result in a loss of benefits.

As noted in Section 405, a worker should file a protective filing statement in January of the year he or she attains full retirement age, even if he or she is working. If a husband or wife may be eligible on the account, the spouse should also file this statement.

If a person who may be eligible as a spouse files on his or her own record, he or she will be required to file as a spouse as well, even if no spouse's benefits are payable because of the husband's or wife's earnings. (see Sec. 302.)

SOCIAL SECURITY TIP

See Section 408 for a discussion of some advantages to starting benefits at a date later than the first possible month of entitlement.

Section 404.5 When to File for Disability Benefits

An application for disability benefits may be filed any time after a worker stops performing *substantial gainful activity*. (see Sec. 504.) Basically, this means that you cannot file for disability benefits until you stop working. There is a full five-month waiting period before any disability benefits are payable. (see Sec. 507.) You may file your application before this waiting period is up, although no benefits will be paid to you until then. It should be noted, however, that for a period of disability to qualify under Social Security, it must be expected to last for twelve months. (see Section 502.) As noted in Sec. 406.2, an application for disability benefits may be retroactive for up to twelve months. To avoid the loss of any monthly benefits, an application for disability benefits should be filed no later than seventeen months after the beginning of disability. The first five months of the disability constitute the waiting period. Because the disability application can be retroactive for twelve months, you will not lose any benefits if the disability application is filed within seventeen months after the disability begins.

If your disability has already ended, you may still apply for disability benefits so long as the application is filed within twelve months of the end of your disability. (see Sec. 508.) However, if you fail to file a disability application because your physical condition limited your activities to such an extent that you could not complete and sign an application, or if you were mentally incompetent, you may file an application for disability within thirty-six months of the end of the period of disability and still receive some benefits.

SECTION 405 WHEN YOU DO NOT HAVE TO FILE AN APPLICATION

In certain cases in which you are already entitled to one kind of benefit and then become entitled to a different type of benefit, you will be automatically changed over to the new kind of benefit without having to file an application. This is called *automatic conversion* and it occurs in three basic cases.

The first case is when you are entitled to spouse's benefits and your spouse dies. If the basis of your entitlement as a wife is because you have a child in your care, you do not have to file an application for mother's benefits. (see Sec. 213.) Mother's benefits are payable to widows who have children in their care. If you are entitled to spouse's benefits based on age, you will be converted to widow(er)'s benefits automatically if you are of full retirement age or older at the time of death of your husband or wife. If you are under full retirement age without a child in your care, your benefit will be automatically converted to widow(er)'s benefits only if you are not entitled to a benefit on your own account. This is because the widow(er) has the option of receiving on his or her own account or on his or her spouse's. (see Sec. 303.)

The second situation in which you can be automatically converted to a new kind of benefit occurs when you are receiving disability insurance benefits and reach full retirement age. You do not have to file a new application for retirement benefits. There will be no change in your benefit amount. You will simply be converted over to the retirement rolls and taken off the disability rolls. The amount of your retirement benefit will be the same as the amount of your disability insurance benefit.

The third situation in which automatic conversion occurs is when a child is entitled to benefits as a dependent and the worker dies. The child will be automatically converted to surviving child's benefits and the benefit amount will be increased accordingly.

SECTION 406 RETROACTIVITY OF APPLICATIONS

An application for Social Security benefits may permit the payment of benefits for months prior to the actual month of filing. This is called retroactivity. The rules vary depending on the type of benefit. Generally, for survivor and retirement benefits, an application cannot be more than six months retroactive—for disability, it is twelve months. However, there is no retroactivity for past benefits that are reduced for age, such as retirement, widow(er), or aged spouse benefits.

The rules for the different kinds of benefits and the different circumstances that affect retroactivity are discussed in the following sections.

Section 406.1 **Retroactivity and Retirement or Survivors**

Applications for these benefits (including dependent) cannot be more than six months retroactive, and sometimes they may have less or no retroactivity. *Retroactivity* means that you can be entitled to benefits for months before the month of filing. If you file a protective filing statement, your formal application is considered filed in the month the protective filing statement is filed, if that is an earlier month. (see Sec. 402.)

Retirement and survivor applications may not be retroactive to a month if benefits for such month are reduced for age. (see Sec. 703.) If they are not reduced for age, either because you are of full retirement age or because they are not subject to age reduction, then the application has full, six-month retroactivity.

Benefits reduced for age are retirement (see Sec. 202), spouses age 63 and older (see Sec. 204.1), and widow(er)s age 60 and over (see Sec. 204.4) if they are paid before full retirement age. (see Sec. 703.) Benefits not reduced for age are spouse with child in care (see Sec. 204.2), mother/father's (see Sec. 204.5), child's (see Secs. 205.1–205.4), and parent's (see Sec. 206). Applications for disabled widow(er)'s benefits (see Sec. 204.6) may be retroactive for up to twelve months, the same as applications for regular disability benefits. (see Sec. 406.2.)

Example: Harry reaches full retirement age in January; his wife Wanda is age 63. They both file their applications in July. Neither Harry nor Wanda has earnings over the applicable limits. (see Sec. 801.) Harry's benefits can begin with January because this is no more than six months before the month of filing and the retroactive benefits are not reduced for age because he is at full retirement age. Wanda's benefits cannot start before July, the month of filing, because the retroactive benefits would be reduced for age. (see Sec. 703.) If she had filed a protective filing statement in January, her benefits could begin as of January, even though the application was not filed until July.

Spouses and Widow(er)s

Spouses' benefits are subject to withholding due to the worker's earnings; but even so, the application for a spouse's benefits cannot be retroactive if he or she is under full retirement age unless his or her own earnings would require offset against his or her monthly benefits. If he or she has no earnings, the application cannot be retroactive if he or she is under full retirement age, even if the spouse's can be. If entitled as a spouse on the basis of having a child in care (see Sec. 204.2), the application may be fully retroactive (six months) because this type of spouse's benefit is not reduced for age.

Widow(er)s' benefits for those age 60 and over (see Sec. 204.4) are reduced for age if taken before full retirement age and, therefore, applications may not be retroactive if benefits would be reduced for past months. An exception is for the widow(er) who files in the month after the month of the worker's death. The application may be retroactive only one month. If the application is filed in the second or later month after the month of death, it may not be retroactive. If the widow(er)'s earnings require offset against benefits, the application may be retroactive in the same way as applications for retirement benefits.

Section 406.2 **Retroactivity and Disability**

An application for disability insurance benefits or disabled widow(er)'s benefits can be retroactive for up to twelve months. This means if you were otherwise eligible for disability benefits within the twelve months before the month you file your application, you may be paid for them. You may not be paid for months before the twelve-month period before the month you file your application.

Example: You become disabled on January 11. No benefits are paid for the first five full months of disability (see Sec. 507), so for February through June, no benefits will be payable (January does not count because it is not a full month of disability). Beginning with July, benefits could be payable. Assume you did not apply for disability until September of the following year. Because the application can be retroactive for only twelve months, the first month for which you can receive disability benefits would be September of the previous year. When your claim is approved, the first payment will include payment for September of the previous year to date. You will lose the benefits for July and August of the previous year.

Applications for child's or spouse's benefits on the account of a wage earner who is entitled to disability insurance benefits are also entitled to the twelve-month retroactivity, with the exception of Spouse's Benefits—Age 62 and Over (see Sec. 204.1), if the wife or husband is under full retirement age. In this case, the rules in Sec. 406.1 apply. If you were disabled in the past but have recovered and returned to work, you may still apply for the disability benefits for the past months you were disabled but only for those months within the twelve months of the date you file your applications. (see Sec. 508.)

There is an exception to the twelve-month retroactivity rule for applying for a period of disability. If you were mentally incompetent or your physical condition limited your activities so that you could not complete and sign an application, you may file for a period of disability within thirty-six months of the end of the disability. Although no benefits can be paid more than twelve months retroactively, if a period of disability is established, a *freeze* can be placed on your earnings record. (see Sec. 503.)

SECTION 407 **RULES ON MEDICARE ENROLLMENT**

To be eligible for Medicare coverage, you must be age 65 or have been disabled and receiving Social Security benefits (including disabled widow's and disabled adult children) for twenty-four months. This is in addition to the full five-month waiting period. In other words, at the time you receive your 25th Social Security disability check, you will be eligible for Medicare coverage. For those disabled with a primary or secondary diagnosis of Amyotrophic Lateral Sclerosis (ALS), also called Lou Gerhig's Disease, Medicare coverage begins with the *first* month of diability benefits entitlement. Medicare coverage is also available for those who are on kidney dialysis. (see Chapter 12.)

As noted in Chapter 12, Medicare has three parts—*hospital insurance, medical insurance,* and *prescription drug coverage.* (see Sec. 1203.1.) These are referred to as Part A (hospital insurance), Part B (medical insurance), and Part D (prescription drug coverage).

You may apply for Medicare hospital insurance (Part A), at any time after you are eligible. An application for this part of Medicare coverage can be retroactive for no more than six months. If you are receiving monthly benefits when you first become eligible, you will be enrolled automatically.

The rules are very different when it comes to medical insurance (Part B). This part of Medicare covers doctors' bills. (see Sec. 1203.)

You must apply for Part B before your first month of eligibility to be covered at the earliest time. *Medical Insurance* is optional. You must pay a premium for it even if you are entitled to regular monthly benefits. If you are receiving benefits at the time you become eligible, you will be notified a few months before that Social Security will automatically enroll you in medical insurance and will start deducting the premiums from your benefit checks. If you are not entitled to monthly benefits at the time you turn age 65, you must make the application for medical insurance yourself.

If you apply for medical insurance (also called *Supplementary Medical Insurance*) before the month you turn age 65, coverage will begin on the first day of the month in which you turn age 65. If you apply for medical insurance during the month you turn age 65, it will become effective on the first day of the following month. If you apply the month after you turn age 65, your coverage will begin the third month after you are age 65. Filing the second month after age 65 grants you coverage starting the fifth month after you are age 65. Filing in the third month covers you starting in the sixth month after your 65th birthday.

If you do not apply for medical insurance within three months after the month you turn 65, then you are limited as to when you can apply for it and when it can begin. The period of time around your 65th birthday, including the month of your 65th birthday, the four months before your 65th birthday, and three months after your 65th birthday, are referred to as the *initial enrollment period*. If you do not apply for medical insurance during that time, then you can only apply during the first calendar quarter of any year thereafter. This is the *general enrollment period*. That would be January, February, and March of the following calendar year. If you miss your initial enrollment period and then you apply for the medical insurance during a general enrollment period, medical insurance coverage will not become effective until July 1st of that year. Additionally, if you have gone twelve months or more without having medical insurance coverage after the month you first could have been eligible, the premium that you pay for medical insurance will be increased. (see Sec. 1203.)

If you did not enroll in Part B (medical insurance) because you were covered by an employer's group health plan, you are entitled to a *special enrollment period*. (see Sec. 1204.) This is a seven-month period beginning with the first month your group coverage ends. You may enroll in Part B during this time. If you enroll in the first month, your Part B coverage begins with the first day of that month. You should do this to avoid a gap in coverage. If you enroll in a later month of the special enrollment period, your coverage begins with the first day of the next month. If your group coverage ends before the end of a month, that month will be considered the first month of your special enrollment period if you sign up for Part B during that same month. In this way you will not have any gap in coverage. Otherwise, the first month will be the next month (the first full month you are not covered by the group plan).

You are also entitled to a special enrollment period near the time you turn age 70 because your employer is not required to cover you after age 70. The special enrollment period for this begins with the third month before the month you turn age 70 and lasts seven months. If you enroll during one of the first three months, your Part B coverage begins with the month you turn age 70. If you enroll in the month you turn age 70 or a later month, coverage begins the first day of the month after the month you enroll. To avoid any gap in coverage, you must enroll before the month you turn age 70.

NOTE: *The Social Security Administration considers you to turn age 70 the day before your 70th birthday. This is important if your birthday is on the first day of the month. If you lose group coverage* *in the month you turn age 70 or earlier, the rules stated in the first two paragraphs of this section will apply if that will give you coverage earlier.*

To be eligible for the special enrollment period, you must be covered both by hospital insurance (Part A) and the group plan in at least one month. If you are not already covered by Part A, you must apply for it. The application may be retroactive for no more than six months. For this reason, if you do not have Part A, you must file before the seventh month of the special enrollment period.

You are limited to one special enrollment period if you did not enroll in Part B when you were first eligible for it (*i.e.*, during your initial enrollment period). If you did enroll then, but later cancelled, you may have more than one special enrollment period only if you were covered by both Part A and a group plan when you cancelled Part B. Additionally, you must enroll in Part B during a special enrollment period each time you lose group coverage.

These rules also apply if you have group coverage based on your spouse's employment, regardless of your spouse's age.

SOCIAL SECURITY TIP

Even if you do not plan to retire, you should contact your local Social Security Office before the month you turn age 65 so you can apply for Medicare without losing any coverage or having to pay any additional premiums.

SECTION 408 WHEN TO START YOUR BENEFITS— THE MONTH OF ELECTION

Applications for monthly benefits may, in certain circumstances, be retroactive. This means that you may start your legal entitlement beginning in a month before the month you file your application. For retirement or widow's benefits, the month you choose your legal entitlement to benefits to begin is called the *month of election*.

There is usually no disadvantage to beginning your legal entitlement at the earliest possible time. However, there are some exceptions to this rule.

If you are self-employed, you should consider a special rule that excludes self-employment income from earnings for purposes of the retirement test. (see Sec. 808.) Self-employment income received after your first year of entitlement, but attributable to services before the month of entitlement, will not be included as countable earnings for the later year.

Example: Jim is a self-employed plumber who turns age 63 in July 2007. He expects $36,000 net earnings for that year and $36,000 net earnings for 2008. Of his expected 2008 earnings, $10,000 will result from services rendered in 2007 but before December 2007. When planning for his Social Security filing (he should be doing this in or before January to fully protect his rights), he learns that based on his expected 2007 earnings and his benefit amount of $1,200 a month, he could receive $2,880 in benefits for 2007 with a January month of election.

However, because of the special exclusion rule, he will be better off with a December 2007 month of election, even though he loses the $2,880. With a December 2007 month of election he can exclude from the following year's countable earnings the $10,000 he expects to receive in 2008 attributable to services rendered before December 2007. This means his 2008 countable earnings will be only $26,000. Under the 1-for-2 rule by which he loses $1 in benefits for every $2 over the annual limit, he will receive $5,000 more benefits in 2008 than if his countable income were $36,000. (see Sec. 801.) By not taking the $2,880 in benefits he could receive in 2007, he will get that $2,880 in 2008 plus an extra $2,120 in benefits for 2008, a 74% return on his money.

If your earnings are high enough to prevent payment of benefits, but you are eligible for a *nonservice* month (see Sec. 804), you may wish to forego this benefit if you will have more *nonservice* months in a later year and wish to use them then. Generally, you are eligible for *nonservice* months in only one year.

Example: Bill is a merchant who earns $120,000 a year and does not plan to retire. However, in 2007, he will not work in July and may be eligible for benefits for that month. In 2008, he will have the same annual earnings, but will not work in February, July, or August. Clearly, he is better off if he receives benefits for the three *nonservice* months in 2008, rather than only one in 2007. To do this, his first month of entitlement must be later than July 2007. (If he is eligible for Medicare earlier, he may restrict his filing for Medicare only. (see Sec. 404.2.))

At one time, you could not change the *month of election* that you chose at the time you filed your application unless you withdrew the application. Now, the month of election is conditional and can be changed at a later date so long as the new month of election is within the retroactive life of the application. (see Sec. 406.1.)

You will require the assistance of a claims representative to figure out what your best month of election should be in close cases. When you visit your district office to discuss this, make sure that you have as accurate an estimate of annual earnings as possible.

SOCIAL SECURITY TIP

Make sure that you file a protective filing statement with your district office in January of any year in which you will be 62 so that you may take advantage of a January month of election if that would result in extra benefits payed to you.

If you go to your district office to get a benefit estimate and to discuss this question, make sure that your last two years' earnings are included in the estimate (bring your W-2 forms or tax returns) and that your estimated earnings are as accurate as possible. (see Sec. 1403.)

For a complete discussion of the choices that a widow or widower who is entitled to a widow or widower's benefit as well as a benefit on her own account must make, see Section 303.

SECTION 409 REQUIRED DOCUMENTS— IN GENERAL

You will need different documents depending on what type of claim you file. These are discussed in more detail in the following sections. Social Security always requires original documents. You cannot make a photocopy of a birth certificate or W-2 form. It will not be accepted by Social Security without the original.

Sometimes clerks of Vital Statistics Offices will give you a photocopy birth certificate. If this is the case, make sure that the photocopy has an original raised seal or is stamped and signed by the clerk. This is what is referred to as an *original copy*.

When you bring your documents into the Social Security office, they will make their own photocopies and return the documents to you. You cannot give them the photocopies in the first place—they must see the actual original documents.

Sometimes people delay filing a claim for benefits because they do not have all of their required documents together. This could be a very bad mistake that could result in a loss of benefits.

> *Caution:* Do not wait to gather all of your documents together before filing your claim.

Although it is a good idea to have the documents on hand when you file, it is not a good idea to delay filing. You can file an application and submit the documents at a later time.

Sometimes Social Security will get them for you. It is important that your application be filed at the earliest possible time so that you may receive all the benefits to which you are entitled. If you are late in filing the application, you may lose benefits. Of course, if you have your documents together when you file your claim, this will speed up the processing, but the processing of the claim can begin even without all the documents. Try to get your documents together well before you intend to file your claim, but when it comes time to file, do not delay—even if you do not have them all.

Section 409.1 Required Documents for Filing a Retirement Claim

When you file a claim for retirement benefits, you will need your birth certificate or other acceptable proof of age. (see Sec. 410.) You will also need all W-2 forms for the last two years. The W-2 forms are the statements of earnings issued by each employer and show the total amount of your annual earnings. The reason you need these documents is that Social Security's records of earnings are behind by at least one year—sometimes two years. These W-2 forms will establish your earnings so that they can be used in figuring your benefit. Please note that if you had more than one employer, you should make sure you bring a W-2 from each one. Also, some people receive W-2 forms from a union or some other source of earnings. Make sure you bring these as well.

If you are self-employed, you will need the last two or three years' income tax returns for yourself as well as for your business. (see Sec. 412.)

Section 409.2 **Required Documents for Filing a Spouse's Claim**

When you file a husband's or wife's claim, whether because you are age 62 or because you have children in your care, Social Security will require your birth certificate. However, a marriage certificate is not required. Instead, Social Security will require your husband or wife to sign a form that certifies that you are presently married.

NOTE: *If you are filing an application on your own earnings record as well, you should bring your last two years' W-2 forms (if you have worked within the last two years). (see Sec. 409.1.) If you are filing as a divorced spouse, you will need your marriage certificate and final divorce decree. (see Sec. 204.3.)*

Section 409.3 **Required Documents for Filing a Widow(er)'s Claim**

When you file a claim for widow(er)'s benefits, you will need your spouse's death certificate, your own birth certificate, and your marriage certificate. If you are filing as a surviving divorced spouse, you will also need your divorce papers. Additionally, if your husband or wife had worked within the last two years, you will need his or her W-2 forms from all his or her employers.

NOTE: *If you were receiving spouse's benefits, you may not have to file a new application. (see Sec. 405.)*

Section 409.4 **Required Documents for Filing a Child's or Parent's Claim**

When filing a child's claim, you will need a birth certificate for each child. If the child is a stepchild, the marriage certificate of the natural parent to the worker will also be required to establish the relationship. For adopted children, the adoption papers will be required. For illegitimate children, it will have to be proven that the father acknowledged the child as his own before he became entitled to Social Security benefits or before he died. The proof can take the form of signing a report card as the father or signing for the hospital bill at the time of the birth of the child or other such documents—any written acknowledgment will suffice.

In the case of a person filing as a grandchild, there must be proof of death (a death certificate) or disability of both parents, as well as birth certificates of the grandchild and the parents to establish the relationship to the worker. Disability will not be something you can get in a document. You must supply names and addresses of treating doctors and hospitals. Social Security will obtain the records.

Section 409.5 **Required Documents for Filing a Disability Claim**

Medical evidence or medical requirements are not discussed in this section, only documents that must be produced at the time the application is filed. For a person who is filing for disability benefits on his or her own account, a birth certificate will be required if you are born in the year 1930 or later, or if you are age 59½ or older at the time the application is made. Proof of age if you were born in 1930 or later is required because there is a special insured status requirement for persons who turn age 22 after 1951. It is the Social Security Administration's policy to obtain a birth certificate for persons who are 59½ or older at the time of the application so they can be changed over to the retirement benefits at full retirement age without having to recontact the beneficiary for proof at that time.

The Social Security Administration will not require you to submit any documents in connection with the disability claim until such time as your claim is allowed on the medical evidence. Most disability cases are denied. Therefore, Social Security does not go out of its way to get documents or to require you to get documents until the claim is allowed on medical grounds. If you have the documents, you should submit them when you file, because if they are in the file, Social Security can pay you benefits as soon as the claim is allowed. Otherwise, they may have to contact you again after the claim is allowed to obtain the necessary documents.

SECTION 410 PROOF OF AGE RULES

Most Social Security beneficiaries receive benefits on the basis of their age. The Social Security Administration (SSA) has very precise guidelines and requirements for proof of age. The SSA will not accept just anything.

The SSA classifies different kinds of proof of age into two basic categories—primary evidence and secondary evidence. The SSA considers *primary evidence* of age to be either a birth certificate or a baptismal certificate recorded before the age of five.

Usually a birth certificate or a baptismal certificate will contain not only the date of your birth but also the date that the document was first recorded. Sometimes a birth certificate is not recorded until years after a person's birth. If your birth or baptismal certificate was not recorded within five years of birth, it will not be accepted as primary evidence. Please note that you do not need a baptismal certificate *and* birth certificate; either one will do. If you do not happen to have a birth certificate or a baptismal certificate with you at the time you file your application, the SSA will not accept other evidence of your age unless there is a satisfactory explanation of why there is no primary evidence.

If you were not baptized, obviously you cannot be expected to have a baptismal certificate. However, if you claim that there is no birth certificate for you, the SSA may require a statement to that effect from your state's Bureau of Vital Statistics. Some states did not record births years ago and the SSA has a list of all states that shows whether or not they recorded births. If the state in which you were born did not record births at the time you were born, that will be satisfactory evidence of the unavailability of a birth certificate. However, if your state did record births at the time you were born, the SSA generally will require some proof that there is no birth certificate. Such proof would be a statement from the Bureau of Vital Statistics of your state that they searched for your birth certificate and could not find one.

If there is no primary evidence, then the SSA will consider what is referred to as *secondary evidence*. Secondary evidence includes such things as a birth certificate or baptismal certificate recorded more than five years after birth, passports, census records, marriage certificates that show your age, immigration records, and so forth. (See Appendix A for a listing of types of secondary evidence the Social Security Administration will consider.)

Additionally, when you applied for your Social Security number, you were asked to give your date of birth, and Social Security still has that information. If you submit one piece of secondary evidence listed in Section II-1 through II-2 of the list in Appendix A and it agrees with the date of birth you gave when you applied for a Social Security card, no further evidence will be required. However, if you submit two or more pieces of evidence that contain different dates of birth, or if there is any discrepancy between the date of birth you gave when you filed for your Social Security number and any secondary evidence, then the SSA will require full development of secondary evidence. In this event, they will attempt to get as much of the evidence listed in Appendix A as possible, and then they can make a determination to establish your date of birth.

When considering the different kinds of secondary evidence, they will generally consider as best that evidence that is oldest and that is least likely to be subject to error. For instance, a birth certificate recorded at age seven would be considered very good secondary evidence, because it was recorded early in life and for a purpose that generally would require that exact date of birth. Date of birth on a marriage certificate or an employment record generally is not considered very good evidence, because it is usually recorded later in life and the purpose for which it is recorded does not require the exact date of birth.

If there is a piece of evidence that shows your date of birth as being younger, such as an employment record or your date of birth on your Social Security card, you will be asked to explain why it is different. Many people gave a different date of birth when they applied for a Social Security number. Perhaps the employer took the Social Security number application form and they wanted the employer to think they were younger. If you did something like that, do not be afraid to tell it to a representative. They will not hold it against you. They are only looking to resolve the discrepancies in the evidence.

SECTION 411 PROOF OF MARRIAGE RULES

When you are required to establish your marriage to be entitled to benefits, the Social Security Administration may require your marriage certificate. Marriages are usually recorded, so there must be an explanation if you cannot obtain one. You will usually be required to produce a statement from the Bureau of Vital Statistics to the effect that a search was made for your marriage and that no record was found. If there is no record of your marriage, you may establish it by secondary evidence. The oldest and best evidence is recorded for a purpose that would require information about marriage, such as a passport or a child's birth certificate that shows the names of the parents. Statements from your spouse's relatives may also be obtained. (see Sec. 210.)

SECTION 412 **SPECIAL PROBLEMS FOR BUSINESS OWNERS**

If you own your own business, whether you are self-employed or whether you have set it up as a corporation, you can encounter special problems when you claim retirement benefits from Social Security. If you are closing up your business altogether or you are selling it to a third party who is not related to you, and you will have no further involvement in the business, you should not have a problem. However, Social Security almost always requires a face-to-face interview if you own your own business. You cannot usually file a claim over the phone. The reason for this is that the Social Security Administration (SSA) wants to question you in detail about your business and determine how credible you appear. The interviewer will make a written determination about whether or not he or she believes you are telling the truth.

If you are not selling your business outright to a nonrelative or you are not closing up shop altogether but you are claiming retirement benefits based on a decrease in earnings, you will have to give a complete and thorough explanation as to why your earnings are decreasing. It is not enough to simply cut your salary down on the books. That means absolutely nothing to Social Security. They will want to know what duties you are performing now that you are claiming partial retirement. They will want to see whether or not the earnings that you report are consistent with the duties you perform. They will want to know who is performing the other duties that you are no longer doing and what qualifications they have for this. It is not enough to say simply, "My wife will run the business" if she has never been involved in the operation of the business.

If you tell the SSA that you will not go to work on certain days, you can be sure that they will send somebody to your place of business on those days to confirm that you are not there. A Social Security representative may pose as a customer.

You will also be asked to give the names and addresses of your major customers and suppliers, because the SSA will contact them to verify that you are no longer dealing with them or that your business is closing.

Social Security will require your own personal tax returns for the last two or three years, as well as the business tax returns. They will want to see whether or not you are taking income from the business and calling it something other than earnings. For instance, if your business is in the corporate form and your salary is cut but your dividends from the business increase, they will look to see why that is or whether you may be disguising salary as dividends. They will also look at your deductions to see if any of them are being overstated to hide income. When you make your initial application, the SSA will take a very detailed statement from you as to the operation and management of your company. Be prepared when you make your application to give a full and complete explanation and to thoroughly explain why your earnings will be less than they were before.

Section 413 **Processing Time Frames**

In general, it takes about two weeks for an application to be processed to payment. At times it can take as little as one week. Unfortunately, in rare cases it can take months and some of those rare cases can take four or five months. Delays can occur if there is a problem with proof of your age or some other requirement, such as marriage. If your first check does not arrive within three months of the time you gave the Social Security Administration all the information and documents required, you may have a right to what is called an *expedited payment*. (see Sec. 1013.)

NOTE: *Checks will not be paid until they are due. If you file early, you will not receive your first check until after the month for which the first payment is due.*

Checks are paid in arrears. (see Sec. 1003.) This means that, for instance, the July check is paid in August. The check you receive in a month is payment for the prior month. If your first month of eligibility will be September and you have made your application in June, you will not receive your first check until October. If your first month of eligibility is September and you made your application in September, you should expect your first check no later than ninety days after you submitted the last evidence required.

The reason that some cases can be processed to payment within two weeks while others take two or three months is that the SSA has a special computer system that can allow the personnel in the local district office to make the computer entries to pay the case. However, not all cases can fit within this computer system, and some cases require approval in a Program Service Center. (see Sec. 102.) This usually adds to the processing time.

SECTION 414 **WITHDRAWAL OF APPLICATION**

You can withdraw an application you have filed at any time before a determination is made on the application. If the Social Security Administration (SSA) has already made a determination on the application, it can only be withdrawn if any other person who would lose benefits because of the withdrawal consents to it in writing and all benefits that have already been paid on the application are returned to the SSA. If the SSA approves a request to withdraw an application, it will be treated as though it were never filed.

A request for a withdrawal of an application must be in writing and filed at the district office. The usual case in which someone wants to withdraw an application occurs when he or she has applied for reduced retirement benefits before full retirement age. He or she later resumes working or earns more than anticipated, so no benefits are payable due to the amount of his or her annual earnings. In that case, it would be advantageous to withdraw the application so that the reduction for age would be eliminated in the event that benefits later became payable before full retirement age. At full retirement age, your benefit will be refigured to exclude the reduction factor for any months for which you did not receive a full monthly benefit. (see Sec. 704.3.)

You may also wish to withdraw an application if you use a *nonservice* (see Sec. 804) month in one year, but may be eligible for more *nonservice* months in a later year. (see Sec. 408.)

Eligibility for Medicare coverage is not affected by withdrawal of an application.

DISABILITY BENEFITS— SPECIAL PROVISIONS

5

Section 501 Disability Benefits—In General

There are three different kinds of Social Security benefits that are paid on account of disability. The most common and well-known is the disability insurance benefit (DIB). (see Sec. 203.) This is the benefit paid to disabled workers. The amount of the benefit is the same as if you were at full retirement age. To be eligible for the DIB you must be specially insured. (see Sec. 604.) You must have worked long enough to be fully insured and you must have worked in the recent past, generally at least a total of five years within the last ten years, although there are exceptions. (see Sec. 604.)

The other Social Security benefits paid on account of disability are disabled adult child (DAC) benefits (see Sec. 205.3) and disabled widow(er) benefits (DWB). (see Sec. 204.6.) These benefits are paid to children of retired, disabled, or deceased workers, and to widow(er)s age 50 to 59. (see Chapter 2.)

This chapter discusses in detail those special rules that are unique to disability benefits. Specific medical requirements are not discussed because they are too numerous and complicated. An entire book is required to cover those issues. If you should file a claim for disability and be denied, you should retain an attorney to represent you. (see Chapter 13.)

Section 502 Definition of Disability

The law defines disability as the inability to do any kind of *substantial gainful activity* (SGA) for a continuous period of at least one year, or as an impairment that may result in death. (see

Sec. 504.) The cause of disability can be either mental or physical, but it must be medically determinable. This means there must be a medical basis for the condition. *Statutory blindness* is also considered a disability. Statutory blindness is defined as central visual acuity of 20/200 or less in the better eye with the use of glasses or the field of vision limited so that the widest diameter subtends an angle no greater than twenty degrees. The one-year duration requirement also applies to blindness cases.

When evaluating your ability to work, the SSA will consider your age, education, and work experience along with your medical condition. This means that even if your medical condition does not prevent all types of work, you may still be eligible if your background is such that you cannot be expected to obtain the only work you are physically able to do.

Example: A laborer in his late fifties who has a back condition that prevents him from performing his regular job and who has done only this type of work may still have the physical ability to do light work, but the SSA will consider him disabled because of his age and limited work background.

If you believe you are disabled, you should file an application for benefits. If you are denied after your first application, you should consult an attorney. Many cases that are denied at first are won on appeal. The rules regarding the medical requirements are very complex and you should have a lawyer represent you if you appeal. (see Chapter 13.)

SOCIAL SECURITY TIP

The rules on proving disability are very complex. If you are unable to do your regular work, you should file a disability application. If your claim is denied, consult an attorney and consider an appeal.

SECTION 503 EARNINGS RECORD "FREEZE"

When you are entitled to disability insurance benefits (DIB) you are also entitled to what is called a *freeze* because of its effect on your earnings record. The months or years during which you are entitled to a period of disability will not be considered for purposes of calculating benefits. For instance, if you were disabled for five years during your fifties, when you reach retirement age and apply for retirement benefits, the five years of disability will be excluded. This is important because retirement benefits are based on your average earnings over many years. If these years of disability were considered, your average earnings would be much lower because you had no earnings during the disability.

Whenever you are eligible for disability insurance benefits, a freeze is placed on your earnings record for that period. This happens even if no disability benefits are actually paid, so long as you meet all the requirements. It is very rare that you would be eligible without being actually paid. *Eligible* in this section means being officially determined eligible after making an application, as opposed to being potentially eligible. The usual situation in which someone is eligible for a period of disability but no benefits are paid is when the disability is based on blindness and the beneficiary is engaging in substantial gainful activity. (see Sec. 504.3.)

The disability freeze applies to the computation of all benefits, not just retirement. It also applies when determining the number of quarters of coverage required. (see Sec. 601.)

SECTION 504 **SUBSTANTIAL GAINFUL ACTIVITY**

Regardless of your medical condition, if you have done work during a time you claim disability benefits, you will not be eligible if the work is determined to be substantial gainful activity (SGA). The exceptions are if you are in a trial work period (see Sec. 509) or if it is an unsuccessful work attempt. (see Sec. 506.)

Section 504.1 **Employees**

If you are an employee, rather than self-employed, the most important factor in determining whether the work is substantial gainful activity is the amount of your earnings. The SSA has established dollar amounts of earnings to use as guidelines. If the earnings average more than $900 per month (as of 2007), the work is considered SGA. This amount increases slightly each year. (If you have access to the Internet, you may check online at **www.socialsecuritybenefitshandbook.com** for updated information.)

When the SSA considers your earnings, they will disregard any part of your pay that is not based on your actual services. For example, you may be working for an employer who is subsidizing part of your pay, as in the case of some sheltered workshops. The employer may be paying more than your work performance is worth economically. The amount of any such subsidy will be deducted from your earnings for the purpose of using the earnings guides previously discussed. If the employer does not set a specific amount for such a subsidy, the SSA will investigate the circumstances to determine how much of your pay you actually earn and how much represents a subsidy.

Likewise, the SSA will deduct from the amount of your earnings any impairment-related work expenses. These may include attendant care services, medical devices, equipment, prostheses, and similar items or services. Drugs and routine medical services are not deductible unless they are necessary to control the disabling condition to enable you to work. Expenses that are not directly related to the impairment cannot be deducted.

Section 504.2 **Self-Employed Persons**

If you are self-employed, the rules are somewhat different. There are three tests that the SSA uses.

Significant Income and Substantial Services

The work activity is considered SGA if:

- you render services that are significant to the operation of the business and

- if you receive a substantial income from the business.

If you run a one-person business without employees, your services are considered to be significant just by that fact alone. If more than one individual is involved in the business, you will be found to be rendering significant services if you contribute more than half the total time required for management of the business or render management services for more than forty-five hours a month, regardless of the total management time required by the business.

An income from the business is *substantial* if the countable earnings you receive are greater than the earnings guidelines used for employees. Because monthly earnings can fluctuate depending on many variables unrelated to ability, the SSA will average your *countable income* by figuring it over a representative period and then dividing by the number of months in that period. To figure these *countable earnings*, the SSA will deduct from the actual net earnings things such as:

- the reasonable monetary value of unpaid help furnished by a spouse, children, or others;

- impairment-related work expenses;

- business expenses that were incurred and paid by another person or agency;

- the value of things provided to you by another individual even though no actual expense was incurred;

- the value of things paid for by anyone for the things provided you to help run the business; and,

- soil bank payments if you participate in that farming program.

Even if countable income does not average more than the amount referred to in the previous list, you are still considered to be receiving substantial income if the livelihood the business provides to you is:

- comparable to your livelihood before becoming disabled or

- comparable to that of unimpaired self-employed individuals in your community engaged in the same or similar businesses as their means of livelihood.

If your services are not significant or if your earnings are not substantial under this first test, the SSA will look closer at your work activity, using two other tests.

Comparable Work Activity

You will be found to be engaging in SGA if your work activity is comparable to that of unimpaired individuals in the same community engaged in the same or similar businesses as their means of livelihood. The SSA will consider your hours spent working in the business, your skills, energy output, efficiency, duties, and responsibilities. If your work is found not comparable, the SSA will then evaluate the value of your work under the worth of work test.

Worth of Work

You will be found to be engaging in substantial gainful activity if your work activity is clearly worth more than the earnings guidelines for employees, considering its value to the business, or when compared to the salary an owner would pay to an employee for such duties in that business setting.

Section 504.3 **Special Rules for the Blind**

If your disability is based on blindness (see Sec. 502), you will be eligible for monthly benefits even if you are working, as long as your monthly earnings do not average more than $1,500 (as of 2007). Subsidies and impairment-related work expenses may be deducted from the countable earnings as in the case of employees. This amount increases slightly each year. (If you have access to the Internet, you may check online at **www.socialsecuritybenefitshandbook.com** for the most current information.)

If you have shown an ability to earn amounts equal to $1,350 or more, your disability benefits will be terminated. However, if you are age 55 or over, your benefits will not be terminated if your present work is not comparable to the work you did before you became blind. If your new work requires skills and abilities less than or different from those you used before, your benefits will only be suspended for months in which you have earnings over $1,350 or more. (The difference between termination of benefits and suspension is discussed in Chapter 10.)

SOCIAL SECURITY TIP

If your benefits are only suspended and not terminated, then you can have them started again without reapplying and without meeting the one-year duration of disability requirement. (see Sec. 502.)

If you meet the eligibility requirements for disability based on blindness (see Sec. 502), including the work requirement (see Sec. 604), you are eligible for a period of disability, called a *freeze* (see Sec. 503), even if you are performing substantial gainful activity. Although no monthly benefits are paid while you are working or able to work, you are entitled to the advantage of the earnings record freeze. You must file an application for this and meet all the requirements as if you were applying for monthly benefits.

SECTION 505 DATE OF ONSET

The date your disability begins is very important. This date determines how your benefit is computed (see Sec. 702.2) and is used to determine how much work you need to be eligible and when. (see Sec. 604.) It determines when the waiting period (see Sec. 507) begins and whether or not you can receive retroactive benefits. (see Sec. 406.2.)

Your waiting period begins with the first full month of your disability. If you become disabled on the first day of a month, that month will be the first month of the waiting period. If you become disabled on the second or later day of a month, then the next month will be the first month of the waiting period.

Example: If you become disabled on June 10, your waiting period begins with July. If you become disabled on June 1, June is the first month of the waiting period.

The earlier your *date of onset*, the better it is for you. Your waiting period will be used up sooner so that benefits can start with an earlier month. If your onset is an earlier year, you may require fewer work credits and quarters of coverage (see Sec. 604), and your benefit amount will usually be slightly higher. The further back you can go for retroactive benefits (see Sec. 406.2), the more money can be paid for past-due benefits when your claim is awarded.

The date of onset is determined by the date your disability actually began, regardless of whether or not your salary continued.

Example: If you became disabled on June 10, but your salary was paid until December 20, your date of onset is June 10, not December 20, as long as you actually stopped working in June.

If your medical condition started before you stopped working, the time you stopped working is used, not when the condition started. *Work* in this section means *substantial gainful activity*. (see Sec. 504.) If you are disabled and return to work, and then stop again because of the disability, the date of onset will be the second time you stopped work, unless your return to work can be considered an *unsuccessful work attempt*. (see Sec. 506.)

Example: You become disabled for the first time as of January. You are out of work for the entire month of January, but return to your job on February 15 and work until June 15, when you again stop work, this time for good. Unless the work period from February to June is considered an unsuccessful work attempt (see Sec. 506), your date of onset will be July. If the work period from February to June is determined to be an unsuccessful work attempt, your date of onset is January.

If you are out of work for an entire year before returning, you may be entitled to a closed period of disability. (see Sec. 508.)

SECTION 506 UNSUCCESSFUL WORK ATTEMPT

As noted in Sec. 505, the date of onset of your disability is very important. The earlier your onset, the better it is for you. People who have stopped working because of a disability, but have then returned to work before stopping work again, may be able to use the earlier date as the date of onset.

Example: If you become disabled and do not work at all in the month of January, but then return to work in February and work until April 15, when you finally stop working, you may be able to establish January as your date of onset.

A period when you return to work may be considered an *unsuccessful work attempt* if it lasts less than three months and you are forced to stop work again because of the physical or mental conditions imposed by your disability. You must still meet the medical requirements of disability as of the first time you stopped working. The first period of disability must have lasted a full month or longer and there cannot have been any medical improvement during the time you went back to work.

A period of work can still be considered unsuccessful if it lasted longer than three months, as long as all the conditions are present and the work period does not last more than six months. In addition, as a result of the impairment one of the following must be true:

- there must have been frequent absences;

- the work must have been unsatisfactory;

- the work must have been done during a temporary remission; or,

- the work must have been done under special conditions or special considerations given by the employer.

You may have more than one unsuccessful work attempt, as long as there is at least one full month of disability between them and there has been no medical improvement.

Section 507 Waiting Period

There are no benefits payable to either the disabled worker or to any dependents for the first five full months of disability. No benefits are payable during the waiting period, nor will benefits be payable later for any months within the waiting period. No waiting period is required if you were previously entitled to disability benefits within five years of your current disability. The waiting period begins with the first full month of disability after the date of onset. (see Sec. 506.) If you become disabled on the second or later day of the month, that month will not count toward the waiting period.

Example: If you become disabled on April 15, the first full month of disability will be May, and the waiting period will start counting with the month of May, so that May, June, July, August, and September will be the months chargeable to the waiting period. No benefits will be payable for those months. The first month of entitlement to a monthly benefit in that case would be October.

The month you become eligible for the payment of the monthly benefits is called your *date of entitlement.* The waiting period is only used to determine when the monthly benefits should begin. You must still meet the one-year duration requirement mentioned in Sec. 502, unless the disability is expected to result in death. You do not have to wait until the end of the waiting period before filing an application for disability. You may file for disability benefits at any time after you stop working due to disability.

If you file for disability benefits before your waiting period is up, no benefits will be paid until the waiting period has passed. If it appears from the nature of your disability that it will be permanent or will exceed one year, then it is a good idea to file the application as soon as you stop working because the application usually will take two to three months, and often much longer, to be processed and approved. If the waiting period has passed during the time the application is being processed, your benefit checks could begin right away.

Example: You become disabled on April 15, and it appears that your disability will be permanent. The waiting period will be the first five full months of disability—namely May, June, July, August, and September. If you apply for your disability benefits during your waiting period, for example, in June, and it takes three months (until September) for the application to be approved, you will get your first disability check as soon as it is payable. The month of entitlement would be October. You would receive your check on November 3 for October since checks are paid in arrears. (see Sec. 1003.)

Processing time usually takes up to three months or more. If you wait for the waiting period to pass before you make your application, you would be without benefits during the processing time. If the claim is approved, the first payment will include any past-due benefits payable after the waiting period. In the example just discussed, if you waited to apply until November and it took three months (until February) for the claim to be approved, you would be without your benefit payments for those months. But when the first check comes, it will include payment for October, November, December, and January. (see Sec. 1002.)

SECTION 508 CLOSED PERIOD OF DISABILITY

As noted in Section 502, you may be eligible for a disability benefit if your disability lasts for at least one year. An application for disability benefits may be retroactive for up to one year. (see Sec. 406.2.) If you have been disabled for at least one year, but then have returned to work, you may be eligible for disability benefits for the period of disability even if you did not file for the disability benefits at the time. This past period during which you were disabled is referred to as a *closed period* of disability. You will be eligible for the payment of benefits only for months within the twelve-month retroactive life of a disability application. (see Sec. 406.2.)

Example: You become disabled on April 15, 2007, and you recover on June 15, 2008. You return to work at your regular job. You do not file an application for disability benefits until February of 2009. The waiting period starts running from the first full month of disability, which would be May. It runs from May through September. Your first possible month of entitlement to a disability benefit would be October 2007, and your last month of possible entitlement to a disability benefit would be August 2008 (you receive benefits for three months following cessation of the disability, see Sec. 513.)

However, because you did not apply until February 2009, your application can be retroactive for only twelve months, which brings it back to February 2008. Because at the time you apply you have recovered from your disability, the period of time that you were disabled is referred to as a closed period of disability. If the claim is approved, you will be paid retroactive benefits for the months of February 2008 through August 2008. If you had applied for the benefits no later than October 2008, you would have received the benefits for all the months that would be payable, namely from October 2007 (the first month of entitlement) through August 2008.

SECTION 509 **TRIAL WORK PERIOD**

After you have become entitled to disability benefits, you may attempt to work without having your disability benefits immediately terminated if you are still medically disabled. This is referred to as a *trial work period*. It is different from the unsuccessful work attempt discussed in Section 506. The trial work period only applies after you have become entitled to disability benefits, but the unsuccessful work attempt applies to work periods before you apply.

The purpose of the trial work period is to allow a disabled beneficiary who is still physically disabled to try to work without penalizing him or her. Earnings during a trial period have no effect on benefits, even if they exceed the earnings limits that apply to other kinds of benefits. The work test does not apply to disability benefits. (see Sec. 801.)

You are not eligible for a trial work period if you have made a medical recovery from your disability or if your medical condition has changed to the extent that you are no longer totally disabled, even if you are partially disabled. You must still meet all the medical requirements of total disability to be eligible for a trial work period.

If you are still medically totally disabled, then your work, even if it is substantial gainful activity (see Sec. 504), will not be considered in determining whether or not your benefits should be cut off. If the work activity you are performing is not substantial gainful activity, then your benefits will continue. Only months in which you have earnings of more than $580 will count toward the trial work period. If you are self-employed, a trial work period month will be charged if you spend more than eighty hours per month at work, or if your net earnings exceed the $580 figure.

SOCIAL SECURITY TIP

This amount increases slightly each year. If you have access to the Internet, you may check online for updated information at:
www.socialsecuritybenefitshandbook.com

The nine months of the trial work period do not necessarily have to be consecutive. If you use up two months of the trial work period, stop working altogether for a while, then work for another two months, you will have used up four months of the trial work period and will only have five months remaining.

Example: You become entitled to disability benefits in January 2007. In December, you obtain part-time employment and earn $800 per month until March 2008. This work activity is below the earnings guidelines described in Section 504 and therefore does not constitute substantial gainful activity. It has no effect on your disability benefits, but it does use up four of your trial work period months because it is over the trial work period monthly earnings limit.

However, in April 2008 you begin making $1,500 per month. This is substantial gainful activity because it exceeds the earnings guidelines of Section 504. You continue earning $1,500 per month from April

2008 through June 2008. You have now used up seven months of your trial work period. You stop working in June and have no earnings until September 2008, at which time you again begin earning $1,500 per month and you continue earning at that rate from then on. Your trial work period months are December 2007 through June 2008 and September and October 2008. That is nine months.

SOCIAL SECURITY TIP

To be eligible for the trial work period, your medical condition must still constitute a total disability. If your medical condition has improved, you will not be entitled to the trial work period.

You are allowed the nine months for the trial work period within a sixty-month rolling period. Work months outside the rolling period will not count. The SSA applies the sixty-month rule as follows.

When you have completed nine months of the trial work, they will count back sixty consecutive months to see if the nine work months were completed in that sixty-month period. If not, they will disregard the work months that fall before the sixty-month period, and will only count the work months that fall within the sixty-month period. If there are less than nine work months within that sixty-month period, the trial work period continues. Only when nine work months are identified within a sixty-month period will the trial work period be completed.

After this, if you continue working and earning above the substantial gainful activity guidelines (see Sec. 504), then your work activity would mean that you are no longer disabled, regardless of your medical condition. Accordingly, your disability would cease with the first month of substantial gainful activity (see Sec. 504) after the trial work period expires. You receive an additional two checks after the month that your disability is determined to have ceased. (see Sec. 513.)

SECTION 510 REENTITLEMENT PERIOD

The Social Security law is designed to encourage disabled beneficiaries to attempt to return to work. If the beneficiary continues in substantial gainful employment, disability benefits will eventually be terminated. However, there are rules that make it easier to reapply if the disability resumes. The extended period of eligibility and the expedited reinstatement of benefits rules are designed to eliminate delays in getting benefits reinstated after a period of work activity. These provisions are discussed in this section.

Extended Period of Eligibility

The reentitlement period is an additional thirty-six-month period after nine months of trial work, during which you may continue to test your ability to work if you continue to have a disabling impairment. You will be paid benefits for months during this period in which you do not perform substantial gainful activity, but you will not receive benefits for any month after the first three in this period during which you perform such work. If anyone else is receiving monthly benefits based on your earnings record, that individual will not be paid benefits for any month for which you cannot be paid benefits during the reentitlement period.

If your benefits are stopped because you perform substantial gainful activity, they may be started again without a new application and a new determination of disability if you discontinue doing substantial gainful activity during this period. In determining, for reentitlement benefit purposes, whether you do substantial gainful activity in a month, the SSA considers your work or earnings for only that month. The SSA does not consider the average amount of your work or earnings over a period of months.

Expedited Reinstatement of Benefits

If your disability benefits were terminated because of work activity, you can request reinstatement within sixty months from the month of termination, and the SSA may make provisional payments to you while they decide whether to reinstate your benefits. You must be unable to work because of the original medical condition.

SECTION 511 EFFECT OF WORKERS' COMPENSATION BENEFITS

If you receive Social Security disability benefits and also receive workers' compensation benefits because of an on-the-job disability, your Social Security benefits may be affected.

If the combination of Social Security benefits (including bene-fits for your husband or wife and children) plus the amount of the workers' compensation benefits you receive per month is greater than 80% of your *average current earnings* (ACE), your Social Security benefits will be reduced so that the total will come down to the 80% level. Benefits payable to dependents will be reduced first.

Example: Your Social Security disability benefit is $1,500 and you have a child under age 18 who is entitled to $750. You are also eligible for workers' compensation benefits in the amount of $1,200 per month. The total of these benefits is $3,450. If your average current earnings before your disability were $4,000 per month, then 80% of this is $3,200 per month. Because the combination of the Social Security benefits and the workers' compensation benefits is $3,450 and 80% of the average current earnings is $3,200, the difference, $250, must be subtracted from your Social Security benefits.

When determining the average current earnings, the Social Security Administration considers the gross amount of your prior earnings, not your net amount after deductions. The average current earnings are figured in three different ways. Whichever way will give you the highest average is used.

The first method of figuring the average current earnings is to take the average monthly earnings during any one calendar year within the year of your onset of disability or the five preceding years.

The second method of determining the average current earnings is to take the average monthly earnings in any five consecutive calendar years after 1950.

NOTE: *The five years must be consecutive. You cannot pick any five after 1950—they must follow one after another.*

The third method of determining average current earnings is to take the average monthly earnings of all years used in computing the disability benefit. (see Sec. 702.2.)

Whichever of the three methods produces the highest average per month will be used. It is important to note that for purposes of determining average current earnings, your actual earnings are used even if they exceed the amount of earnings subject to FICA tax for that year. Because your earnings record only shows the earnings in a calendar year that are subject to the FICA tax, it is important if your yearly earnings for a particular year exceeded the FICA maximums to bring this to the attention of the Social Security Administration. (A listing of the FICA maximum for all years is located in Appendix C.)

SOCIAL SECURITY TIP

The workers' compensation offset does not apply if the workers' compensation law under which you are receiving workers' compensation benefits provides that compensation benefits will be reduced by the amount of Social Security benefits you receive.

If the total of the Social Security benefits payable on the individual's earning's record is greater than 80% of the average current earnings, then this higher figure is used to figure the offset instead of the 80% figure.

Example: If the average current earnings are $1,000 per month, 80% is $800. If the total amount of benefits payable on the account, including the dependents, is $900 per month, then the Social Security benefits will be reduced so that the combination of workers' compensation and Social Security benefits does not exceed $900.

It is rare that the total Social Security benefits exceed 80% of average current earnings.

SECTION 512 EFFECT OF OTHER KINDS OF BENEFITS OR PAYMENTS

Benefits paid under private disability insurance policies have no effect on Social Security disability benefits. Employee salary continuation will not have any effect, nor will any back pay, retroactive increases past due, commissions, or any other such payments from an employer. Besides workers' compensation discussed in Section 511, the only type of disability benefits that affect your Social Security disability are those that are required by any federal, state, or local law. For example, some states have laws that require employers to pay disability benefits to disabled employees. Such benefits would be used to offset Social Security disability benefits in the same way as workers' compensation. These benefits are added to the amount of workers' compensation and the computation of the offset is then the same. If the statute requiring the special disability benefit provides for an offset for Social Security benefits, then this offset provision does not apply.

SECTION 513 WHEN DISABILITY BENEFITS END

There is a difference between *cessation* of disability and *termination* of disability benefits. Cessation of disability occurs when the Social Security Administration determines you are no longer totally disabled within the definition of disability for Social Security purposes. (see Sec. 502.) Termination of benefits occurs two months after cessation of disability.

Example: If the SSA determines that your disability ceased in June, your disability will terminate as of August so that you will receive the benefits for June, July, and August, but not thereafter.

SOCIAL SECURITY TIP

Cessation of disability occurs when your medical condition is no longer considered to be totally disabling or when you begin performing substantial gainful activity. (see Sec. 504.)

The Social Security Administration (SSA) conducts periodic reviews of many Social Security disability cases to reconsider the medical condition of the beneficiary. If, after such a medical review, the SSA determines that your condition is no longer totally disabling, your disability will be considered to have ceased. It is the policy of the Social Security Administration to send you a notice of this determination, and if they fail to do so, your disability will not be considered to have ceased until such time as you receive the notice.

Example: The Social Security Administration conducts a medical review of your case and determines that based on your medical records, your disability ceased as of June 19. However, because of office problems, they did not mail out the notice to you until August. It is the Social Security Administration's policy to make your official cessation of disability in August, the month you received the notice, rather than June, the month that they determined your medical evidence no longer was considered totally disabling.

Even if your medical condition remains the same or worsens, if you are performing substantial gainful activity (see Sec. 504), your disability will be considered to have ceased.

NOTE: *Not all work activity is considered substantial gainful activity. If you are entitled to a trial work period (see Sec. 509), your work activity will not be considered substantial gainful activity until nine months of the trial work period have passed. You may then be entitled to further benefits for nonwork months. (see Sec. 510.)*

Section 514 Continuing Disability Review

The Social Security Administration (SSA) conducts periodic reviews of disability cases to determine if you are working or if your medical condition has changed. Some cases are reviewed more frequently than others and some cases are not reviewed at all. It depends on the nature of your disability. When your claim is first awarded, a date is usually set at that time for a future review. The SSA will not conduct a review based on work activity alone if you have received benefits for at least twenty-four months. The SSA will still conduct regularly scheduled reviews unless you are using a *ticket to work.* (see Sec. 515.)

You will be notified when your case is being called for review, and generally you will be called to the district office to give current information about any work activity you may be doing, the names of your current doctors, and any recent periods of hospitalization. The Social Security Administration may have you examined by one of its consultant physicians, at its expense. If you medically recover while participating in a vocational rehabilitation program that is likely to lead to your becoming self-supporting, benefits may continue until the program ends.

If you do not cooperate with this continuing disability review, the SSA has the authority to stop your disability benefits because you fail to cooperate.

SECTION 515 **TICKET TO WORK**

This law was enacted to provide health care and employment services to people with disabilities to help reduce their dependence on cash benefit programs. Provisions of the law that involve Social Security include the *Ticket to Work and Self-Sufficiency Program* (Ticket to Work program) that allows Social Security disability beneficiaries to get employment services, vocational rehabilitation services, or other support services that will help them to work. Additionally, people with disabilities will have the option of maintaining coverage while working. The law extends premium-free Medicare Part A (hospital insurance) coverage to eight and a half years, including the trial work period, for beneficiaries who work.

Eligible Social Security disability beneficiaries will receive a *ticket* they may use to obtain vocational rehabilitation, employment or other support services from an approved employment network or state vocational rehabilitation agency of their choice. The Ticket to Work program is voluntary for beneficiaries and employment networks.

When disability benefits stop because of work activity, the beneficiary can request reinstatement of benefits, including Medicare, without having to go through the difficult process of filing a new application. To be eligible for expedited reinstatement:

- you must be unable to work because of your medical condition;

- your impairment must be the same or related to the impairment that was the basis for your previous disability benefits; and,

- you must file the request for reinstatement within sixty months from the month your benefits are terminated.

This time limit may be extended for good cause. In addition, you may receive provisional benefits, including Medicare, for up to six months while your case is being reviewed. If you are found not disabled, the benefits typically will not constitute an overpayment.

If you are using a ticket (a document that the SSA issues for participation in the program), you will not be subject to continuing disability reviews. However, benefits may be stopped if your earnings are above the substantial gainful activity level. Beneficiaries who have been receiving benefits for at least two years will not be medically reviewed just because they are working. The law also requires the SSA to staff work-incentive specialists to provide information about employment support programs to beneficiaries who want to work.

In general, you must be 18 years of age or older and under age 65 to be eligible for a ticket. You may receive only one ticket during a period of disability. If your benefits cease but you become reentitled, you may receive another one. The ticket will terminate when you reach age 65. You will no longer be able to obtain employment or vocational services when the ticket terminates.

If you are not making timely progress in preparing for self-supporting work, the SSA may conduct a continuing disability review that may find that you are no longer medically disabled. If you are making timely progress, such reviews will not be done. *Timely progress* rules require that you actively participate in an employment plan during the first two years after the month you begin using the ticket and also require an increase in your work activity and earnings during the next two years. This means you must work at least three months within the first three years and at least six months in the fourth year. You must earn at least as much as the earnings level for determining nonblind substantial gainful activity. (see Sec. 504.1.)

INSURED STATUS— WORK REQUIREMENT 6

SECTION 601 WORK REQUIREMENT—IN GENERAL

To qualify for a Social Security benefit, either you or the person on whose earnings record you claim benefits must have worked a certain amount of time in employment covered by Social Security. Almost all employment in the United States is now covered. The work requirement is called *insured status.*

There are different kinds of insured status depending on the type of benefits being claimed. *Fully insured* status (see Sec. 602) is required for most benefits. *Currently insured* status (see Sec. 603) is required for Mother/Father Benefits with Child in Care (see Sec. 204.5) and Child's Benefits. (see Secs. 205.1–205.4.) A special *disability insured* status (see Sec. 604) is required for disability insurance benefits. (see Sec. 203.)

Dependents and survivors are eligible based on relationship to an insured worker. There is no work requirement for them. The person on whose account benefits are claimed must meet the applicable insured status requirement.

The eligibility requirements for the different kinds of benefits are listed in Section 202–208. Each listing states the insured status requirement for that particular benefit. If you have insured status on your own and also qualify as a dependent or survivor, you may be entitled on both accounts. (see Chapter 3.)

The insured status requirement does not affect the amount of the benefit. It sets a minimum work requirement that must be met before any benefit is payable. Once this minimum is met, a benefit amount is computed based on average earnings. (see Chapter 7.)

Insured status is gained by earning *quarters of coverage*. (see Sec. 605.) These are calendar quarters for which credit is given based on certain minimum earnings during the year.

SECTION 602 FULLY INSURED STATUS

Fully insured status is required for most benefits. To be fully insured for retirement benefits, you must earn forty quarters of coverage. (see Sec. 605.) For survivor and disability benefits, you must earn one quarter of coverage for every year after the year you turn age 22, up to and including the year you become disabled (for disability insurance benefits) or die (for survivor benefits). There is an additional requirement for disability insurance benefits (see Sec. 604) and certain survivor benefits do not require fully insured status. (see Sec. 603.)

Social Security rules provide that you attain your age on the day before your birthday. If your birthday is on January 1, you attain age 22 in the year before that birthday for purposes of figuring the insured status requirement.

To collect spouse's, widow(er)'s, or child's benefits, you do not have to meet the work requirement yourself. Instead, you must be the spouse, widow(er), or child of a worker who meets the requirement.

SOCIAL SECURITY TIP

The minimum number of *quarters of coverage* required in any case is six. The maximum is forty.

Example: John was born August 11, 1950. He became disabled on June 5, 1994. Adding 22 to the year of birth (22 + 1950 = 1972), John attained age 22 in 1972. Subtracting 1972 from the year of onset of disability (1994 − 1972 = 22), John needs 22 quarters of coverage to meet the fully insured part of disability insured status. (see Sec. 604.)

See Charts 2 and 3 in Appendix B for quarters of coverage required for disability/survivor insured status and special disability insured status.

SECTION 603 CURRENTLY INSURED STATUS

This type of insured status requires fewer quarters of coverage (see Sec. 605) than fully insured status. (see Sec. 602.) However, only some kinds of benefits can be based on currently insured status. These are Child's Benefits (see Secs. 205.1-205.4), Mother/Father Benefits (see Sec. 204.5), the Lump Sum Death Benefit (see Sec. 208), and Medicare for kidney failure cases. (see Sec. 207.1.)

A worker must earn at least six quarters of coverage within the thirteen-calendar-quarter period ending with the calendar quarter of death. The calendar quarters are:

- first quarter—January, February, March;

- second quarter—April, May, June;

- third quarter—July, August, September; and,

- fourth quarter—October, November, December.

To determine this period, take the quarter and year of death and subtract three from the year. The period begins with the quarter of the resulting year, which corresponds to the quarter of death.

Example: Jim died on May 15, 2005. This is in the second quarter of 2005. Subtract 3 from 2005, which equals 2002. The thirteen-quarter period begins with the second quarter of 2002 and ends with the second quarter of 2005. If Jim earned six quarters of coverage during that period, including the beginning and ending quarters, he is currently insured.

SECTION 604 DISABILITY INSURED STATUS

Eligibility for disability insurance benefits (see Sec. 203) requires a special *disability insured status*. You must be fully insured (see Sec. 602) and meet a second requirement of recent quarters of coverage. (see Sec. 605.) This second requirement is different, depending on when you become disabled.

If you become disabled in or after the calendar quarter you reach age 31, you must have at least twenty quarters of coverage during the forty-calendar-quarter period ending with the quarter your disability begins. (see Sec. 505.) To determine this period, subtract 10 from the year the disability begins and begin with the first quarter after the quarter in the resulting year that corresponds to the quarter of onset of disability. The calendar quarters are the same as those for currently insured status. (see Sec. 603.)

Example: John becomes disabled on September 5, 2007. This is the third quarter of 2007. Subtracting 10 from the year equals 1997. The corresponding quarter of that year is the third quarter. The forty-quarter period begins with the first quarter after the corresponding quarter. Therefore, the period begins with the fourth quarter of 1997 and ends with the third

145

quarter of 2007. If John has twenty quarters of coverage within this period, including the beginning and ending quarters, he will meet the second part of the disability insured status requirement.

Sometimes the requirement is referred to as the *five-year rule* or the *five-year out of ten-year rule*. This is somewhat misleading. Although twenty quarters is five years and forty quarters is ten years, the legal requirement is based on quarters, not years. The twenty quarters required do not have to be consecutive; they can be spread out. The forty-quarter period does not always correspond to the beginning and ending of calendar years. This rule is more accurately called the 20/40 rule (*i.e.*, twenty quarters required in the forty-quarter period).

If you become disabled before the calendar quarter of your 31st birthday, there is an alternative to the 20/40 rule. Instead, you must have one quarter of coverage for every two calendar quarters in the period beginning with the calendar quarter after the quarter of your 21st birthday and ending with the quarter of onset of disability. (see Sec. 505.) If the number of quarters in this period is an odd number, use the next lower even number. A minimum of six quarters of coverage is always required. Quarters of coverage earned before age 21 may be used if this is necessary to meet the requirement.

If you were disabled before age 31 and received benefits based on the alternative to the 20/40 rule just discussed, but your disability ceased and you then become disabled again after age 31, you will meet the disability insured status requirement, even if you cannot satisfy the 20/40 rule, if you have at least one quarter of coverage for every two calendar quarters beginning with the quarter after attainment of age 21 and ending with the quarter of the new onset date. You exclude any quarter wholly or partially within the prior period of disability, except the beginning or ending quarters if they are quarters of coverage.

In all cases, you must be fully insured. (see Sec. 602.)

SECTION 605 QUARTERS OF COVERAGE— IN GENERAL

A *quarter of coverage* is a calendar quarter for which credit is given by Social Security for purposes of deciding if a person has worked long enough to qualify for benefits. (see Sec. 601.) A minimum amount of wages from covered employment or self-employment income must be earned to get credit. Almost all employment and self-employment is now covered by Social Security. The amount of earnings required to get credit has changed. (The rules are discussed in the following sections of this chapter.)

Section 605.1 Quarters of Coverage: Pre-1978 for Employees

In years before 1978, you receive a quarter of coverage for each calendar quarter during which you were paid $50 or more. It does not matter when the wages were earned. The quarter of coverage is assigned to the quarter in which the wages were paid to you. However, if you were paid maximum yearly earnings subject to Social Security (the FICA maximum), you are given credit for the four quarters of that year, even if the earnings were paid in less than four quarters. The yearly FICA maximums are listed in Appendix C.

There is a special rule that applies to farm workers for years before 1978. Instead of the $50 per quarter rule, a farm worker received one quarter of coverage for each $100 in cash wages paid during a year, without regard to the quarter in which the wages were paid. Quarters of coverage were assigned beginning with the last calendar quarter and then counting backward.

Beginning in 1978, the rules for all employees were changed. (see Sec. 605.2.) The rules have always been different for the self-employed. (see Sec. 605.3.)

Section 605.2 Quarters of Coverage: Post-1977 for Employees

Beginning with 1978, quarters of coverage are assigned based on total yearly earnings instead of earnings paid within a calendar quarter. A certain amount has been designated for each year and one quarter of coverage is credited for each multiple of that amount that is paid within the year. These amounts are listed in Appendix B, Chart 1.

Example: John was paid $800 in 1984, when the required multiple was $390. He is credited with two quarters of coverage because his earnings are at least two multiples of $390, but less than three multiples. Jim was paid $1,600 in 1984. He receives four quarters of coverage because his earnings are at least four multiples of $390.

No more than four quarters of coverage are given for one calendar year. A quarter of coverage cannot be assigned for any quarter that has not yet started or for any quarter that begins after the worker's death.

Section 605.3 **Quarters of Coverage:**
For the Self-Employed

The method of determining quarters of coverage for self-employed individuals is different from the method for employees. Before 1978, the self-employed person received four quarters of coverage for a year if the net earnings from self-employment were $400 or more. If the net earnings from self-employment were less, the self-employed did not receive any quarters of coverage. It was all or nothing.

Beginning in 1978, the rules changed. For 1978 and all later years, a self-employed person receives quarters of coverage based on the amount of total yearly earnings in the same way as an employee. (see Sec. 605.2.) However, the self-employed individual must still meet a minimum of $400 in net earnings from self-employment to receive any quarters of coverage.

Example: John works as a plumber for the Smith Plumbing Company. He earned $350 in 1978 in wages. He receives one quarter of coverage, because this is more than the minimum required earnings for one quarter of coverage as discussed in Section 605.2. Joe, however, is a self-employed plumber. His net earnings from self-employment in 1978 were $375. He receives no quarters of coverage, even though his net earnings from self-employment are greater than the minimum earnings required for an employee. If he earned $400 in self-employment income in 1978, he would receive one quarter of coverage. If he had earned $400 in net earnings from self-employment in 1977, he would have received four quarters of coverage.

If you are both self-employed and an employee, add your total earnings as an employee and your net earnings from self-employment to determine how many quarters of coverage you will receive using the rule described in Sec. 605.2. However, to count any net earnings from self-employment into the yearly total, they must be at least $400. If the net earnings are less, they are not added in at all.

Example: Joe is both a self-employed plumber and an occasional employee of Smith Plumbing Company. In 1978, he had $400 in net earnings from self-employment and $350 in wages. Combining the two sums equals $750. Using the rule described in Sec. 605.2, he earns three quarters of coverage. If the earnings and self-employment income were reversed, the outcome would be different. If he had $400 in wages but only $350 in net earnings from self-employment, he would receive only one quarter of coverage. The net earnings from self-employment are less than $400 and do not get added in at all—only his wages count. Because his wages are only one multiple of the minimum required for 1978 ($250), he receives only one quarter of coverage.

BENEFIT AMOUNTS 7

SECTION 701 BENEFIT AMOUNTS—IN GENERAL

For obvious reasons, the way that the Social Security Administration (SSA) computes the amount of benefits payable is very important to everyone. This chapter discusses the rules that are used to figure benefits. Discussed are the basic computation, the recomputations due to earnings after you first become entitled to benefits, the reductions for age and for entitlement to other benefits, and the credits given for delayed retirement.

(Deductions because of earnings are discussed in detail in Chapter 8. The method and timing of payments are discussed in Chapter 10.)

SECTION 702 COMPUTATION OF BENEFITS

The most important feature of the Social Security program is the monthly dollar amount paid to beneficiaries. The manner in which these benefits are calculated is prescribed in detail by the Social Security Act. Over the years there have been many different formulas. The basic formula now used for virtually all new beneficiaries is the 1978 Average Indexed Monthly Earnings formula, also called the AIME method. The basic concepts in the calculation of benefits as well as some of the other formulas used in previous years are discussed in the following section. This will provide a basic understanding of how benefits are calculated. It would be necessary to have the exact earnings record of the wage earner as certified by Social Security to compute an actual benefit.

Section 702.1 Primary Insurance Amount

The first step in figuring benefits is to determine the *primary insurance amount* (PIA). All benefits are based on it. The benefit amount for a retired worker at age 65 and for a disabled worker is equal to the primary insurance amount. It is reduced for retirement benefits before age 65 and increased for delayed retirement.

Benefits for spouses, children, and survivors are figured as a percentage of the primary insurance amount. The PIA is the single most important concept for computing benefit amounts.

Section 702.2 **Basic Computation Formula**

The primary insurance amount (PIA) is based on the earnings of the worker on whose account the benefits are claimed. It is used to calculate benefit amounts. Sample benefit amounts for workers with maximum, high, average, and low lifetime earnings are listed in Appendix D.

There is one basic formula used to compute almost all PIAs. Some special formulas, used rarely, are discussed in Section 702.3. The basic formula is described in this section, but is extremely complicated and is almost always done by the SSA's computers rather than manually.

The 1978 amendments to the Social Security Act mandated *indexing* of earnings to adjust earnings of earlier years for inflation occurring now. The first step of the basic computation formula is to index the worker's annual earnings for past years. Each year's earnings are separately indexed. To do this, the SSA first determines the *indexing year.* For retirement cases, this is the second year before the year the worker becomes age 62 (not necessarily the year of retirement). For disability cases, it is the second year before the onset of disability, and for survivor cases, it is two years before the year of death. For example, for a worker who becomes age 62, disabled, or dies in 2006, the indexing year is 2004.

The SSA then determines the *average annual earnings* of all workers for the indexing year and for each past year after 1950. They divide the average earnings of all workers for the indexing year by the average earnings of all workers for each prior year. They multiply the answer for each year by the amount of the worker's earnings for that prior year (but not more than the FICA maximum for that year). The result is the indexed earnings for each prior year. This process is for all years after 1950 up to, but not including, the indexing year. The SSA uses actual earnings, not indexed earnings, for the indexing year and later years.

After the earnings for all years have been indexed (except the indexing and later years), the SSA then determines how many years to use for the computation. For people born before 1930, subtract 1951 from the year they become age 62, begin the onset of disability, or die—whichever is earliest. (People who become disabled at age 64 would still subtract 1951 from age 62 because that is earlier than the onset of disability.) For people born in 1930 or later, add 22 to the year of birth. Subtract that figure from the year they turn age 62, begin the onset of disability, or die. For retirement and survivor benefits, subtract 5. The result is the number of years used, called *computation years*.

For disability benefits, if the onset of disability is:

- ages 26 or younger, do not subtract anything additional;

- ages 27 through 31, subtract 1;

- ages 32 through 36, subtract 2;

- ages 37 through 41, subtract 3;

- ages 42 through 46, subtract 4; and,

- ages 47 or older, subtract 5.

The minimum number of computation years used is 2. The maximum number of computation years is 35.

After determining the number of computation years, the SSA looks at the annual indexed earnings calculated from 1951 through the year before the year for which the benefit is calculated. You may include the year of death in survivor cases. Take the computation years with the highest indexed earnings, and add up the total indexed earnings for those computation years.

When recomputing a retirement benefit to include after entitlement, the number of computation years is the same. If the earnings for the new year are higher than the indexed earnings of the lowest year used in the first computation, substitute the new year's earnings. When you add the new year's earnings into the total, you must subtract the lowest year's indexed earnings.

Once the SSA has determined the total indexed earnings for the computation years, it divides by the number of months in the computation years. These are called *divisor months*. The number of computation years times twelve equals the divisor months used.

SOCIAL SECURITY TIP

The total of the indexed earnings for the computation years used, divided by the divisor months, rounded to the next lower dollar, yields the average indexed monthly earnings.

The primary insurance amount is a certain percentage of the average indexed monthly earnings. This varies depending on the average indexed monthly earnings and on the year for which the computation is being done. For example, for 1992, the percentages are as follows: 90% of the first $387, plus 32% of the excess over $387 up to $2,333 of the average indexed monthly earnings, plus 15% of the average index monthly earnings over $2,333. The dollar amounts at which the percentages change are called *bend points*. The percentages (90%, 32%, 15%) stay the same for each year, but the bend points change annually. They are determined by dividing the indexing year's average total wages of all workers, by the average total for 1977 ($9,779.44), and multiplying the result by $180 and $1,085 to give the two bend points.

The bend points used depend on the first year of eligibility (*i.e.*, the year the worker becomes age 62, disabled, or dies) and remain applicable for later recomputations, even though the recomputation is done in a later year.

Cost-of-living adjustments are added to the primary insurance amount beginning with the year of eligibility, effective with the month of increase. (see Sec. 704.1.)

Once the primary insurance amount is calculated, the benefit amount payable is determined according to the rules explained in this chapter and in the benefit amounts listed for each type of benefit in Chapter 2.

Section 702.3 **Other Computation Formulas**

The basic computation formula discussed in the preceding section applies to almost all beneficiaries. Other computations are used in a very small number of cases.

The 1978 amendments to the Social Security Act changed the basic computation formula to the average indexed monthly earnings method discussed in Sec. 702.2. The general purpose of this change was to take inflation into account, but it also reduced the amount of benefits.

For workers who attained age 62 before 1984, the Social Security Administration (SSA) may use a different formula. This other formula is called the *new-start transitional guarantee*. When using this formula, however, the SSA does not add in earnings from the year you attained age 62 or later. This formula does not use indexed earnings. Instead, it uses the actual earnings. The transitional guarantee formula may result in a higher primary insurance amount in some cases where the last year's earnings were in 1980 or 1981.

If you had been entitled to disability insurance benefits more than a year before your entitlement to retirement benefits, the year of your death in survivor cases, or a second period of disability, you will receive the higher of a primary insurance amount figured under the basic computation formula, or the primary insurance amount upon which your disability benefit was based. In other words, you will not have a lower primary insurance amount than you had while you were disabled.

The Social Security Administration also uses other formulas when there are little or no earnings after 1951. Only a very small number of people will have a higher benefit under these other computation formulas. The SSA will automatically consider all computation formulas and give you the highest one.

Section 702.4 **Effect of Having Years with No Earnings**

As noted in Section 702.2, the years used in figuring the primary insurance amount are the years from 1951 (or the year you turn age 22, if later) through the year before the year you turn age 62. The lowest five years are dropped from that base period. If you have five or less years with no earnings shown on your earnings record, it will have no effect on your computation. However, if you have more than five years with no earnings, then it will affect your computation, because the overall average monthly earnings during the computation will be less.

Generally, if the year with no earnings is a later year, it will have more of an effect than an earlier year. This is because the amount of earnings covered by Social Security have increased over the years, so that recent years' earnings subject to FICA are very high (see Appendix C), although *indexing* has some-what reduced the disparities.

Section 702.5 **How to Double-Check
Your Benefit Amount**

In the vast majority of cases, the Social Security Administration correctly computes your benefit amount, but sometimes mistakes occur. The most common mistake is the failure to include earnings for a given year. If earnings are not shown on your earnings record, it may affect the amount of your average monthly earnings and, therefore, the amount of your benefit.

If you doubt the accuracy of your benefit amount, the first thing to do is go to your Social Security office and ask them to obtain a copy of your earnings record used in the computation of the benefit. It may take them several weeks or a month to obtain this. You should check to make sure that the correct earnings are posted for each year. If there is a year that does not have earnings shown, determine if it makes a difference in the computation of your benefit. If it is one of the five lowest years in the computation period, then it does not matter.

The general rule is that you can correct your earnings record only for the past three years. However, there are some exceptions to this rule. (see Sec. 1405.) If you have a year with no earnings shown that is more than three years in the past, you can ask the SSA to recheck their records in Baltimore. This is called a *scout*. If earnings turn up on the scout, your benefit will be adjusted. If they do not turn up, the SSA may still allow you to correct your earnings record if you have evidence of the earnings, such as W-2 form, pay stubs, or a tax return.

If all your earnings are shown on your earnings record and you still doubt the accuracy of the benefit, you should ask a claims representative (see Sec. 105) to show you how your benefit was computed step by step.

If you are not satisfied, you have the right to request a reconsideration. This is part of the *administration appeals process.* (see Chapter 13.)

SECTION 703 REDUCTIONS FOR AGE— IN GENERAL

In the case of retirement, spouses age 62 and over, widow(er)s age 60 and over, and disabled widow(er)s, your benefit amount will be reduced if you take the benefit before full retirement age. This is age 65 for those born before 1938 (1940 for widow(er)s). The reduction is figured on a monthly basis, not yearly. Beginning in 2003 (but affecting those turning 62 in 2000), full retirement age is gradually increasing, in two-month increments per year, to age 66 by 2009. There will then be an eleven-year pause. The increases will then resume, going to age 67 by 2027. This change affects those persons turning 62 beginning in 2000. The effect of the change is that the benefit at age 62 is reduced more than it had been previously (by $5/12$ of 1 percent for each extra month).

The following chart contains the full retirement age for workers and spouses born after 1937 (for widow(er)s, see Sec. 703.3).

If the birth date is...	then full retirement age is...
1/2/38–1/1/39	65 years and 2 months
1/2/39–1/1/40	65 years and 4 months
1/2/40–1/1/41	65 years and 6 months
1/2/41–1/1/42	65 years and 8 months
1/2/42–1/1/43	65 years and 10 months
1/2/43–1/1/55	66 years
1/2/55–1/1/56	66 years and 2 months
1/2/56–1/1/57	66 years and 4 months
1/2/57–1/1/58	66 years and 6 months
1/2/58–1/1/59	66 years and 8 months
1/2/59–1/1/60	66 years and 10 months
1/2/60 and later	67 years

There are different reduction formulas for retirement, spouse's, and widow(er)'s benefits. These are discussed in detail in the following sections.

Section 703.1 Reduction for Age: Retirement Benefits

If you are entitled to a retirement benefit before the month you reach full retirement age, the benefit must be reduced. The reduction factor goes by months, not by years, so that if your first month of entitlement is the month before full retirement age, the benefit is reduced by one month. If the first month of entitlement is six months before full retirement age, it will be reduced six months, and so forth all the way back to age 62 (but see Section 209 dealing with the *throughout the month* rule).

The legal reduction factor is ⁵⁄₉ of 1% of the primary insurance amount for each month of the first thirty-six months you are entitled to a benefit before the month you reach full retirement age. The factor for each month of reduction in excess of thirty-six months is ⁵⁄₁₂ of 1%. This applies to individuals whose full retirement age is after age 65. A thirty-six-month reduction comes out to 20%, but remember that the reduction factor goes by month, not by year.

Example: If you were born in September 1934, you turned 65 in September 1999. If your entitlement to benefits started in January 1998, your primary insurance amount is reduced by twenty reduction months because that is the number of months before the month you turn age 65. If your primary insurance amount is $500.00, 1% of it is $5.00 and ⁵⁄₉ of 1% is $2.77. Multiply this amount by the number of reduction months. Twenty times $2.77 is $55.40. The monthly benefit amount is $500.00 minus $55.40, or $444.60. If your full retirement age is over age 65, extra reductions are applied for each month over thirty-six. The actual amount payable to you is rounded down to the nearest dollar ($444.00). (see Sec. 705.6.)

A formula is used by the Social Security Administration to figure the monthly benefit amount instead of the this method.

The formula is 180 minus the number of reduction months, times the primary insurance amount, divided by 180, or:

$$[(180 - RM) \times PIA)]/180.$$

Example: Applying the facts from the previous example, take 180 and subtract 20, the number of reduction months. This leaves 160. Multiply 160 by the primary insurance amount of $500.00 to get 80,000. Divide 80,000 by 180 and the answer is $444.44. This is rounded down to the nearest dollar for a final benefit amount of $444.00.

A third method of figuring the reduced benefit is to use the reduction factor listed on the chart in Appendix E.

Example: The factor for twenty reduction months is .888. Using the same example, .888 times 500 (the primary insurance amount) arrives at a monthly benefit amount of $444.00.

NOTE: *There are some minor discrepancies in the results obtained by using the three formulas. The first formula is from the Social Security Act, the second is the one the SSA uses, and the third is published in Social Security Administration pamphlets.*

Any reduction for age stays in effect until you reach full retirement age. At that time, the reduction factor is readjusted to exclude any reduction for the months before full retirement age for which you do not receive a full monthly benefit. (see Sec. 704.3.) If you receive all monthly benefits, the reduction stays in effect for life.

Section 703.2 **Reduction for Age: Spouse's Benefits**

Benefits payable to a spouse of a retired or disabled worker are reduced if entitlement to the spouse's benefit begins before the month the spouse reaches full retirement age. (See Section 703 for the new rules for those turning age 62 in 2000.) Extra reduction months are applied for months in excess of thirty-six. The reduction factor for these excess months for spouse's benefits is the same as for retirement benefits (*i.e.*, $5/12$ of 1%).

NOTE: *If the spouse is entitled because he or she has a child in care (see Sec. 213), there is no reduction for age.*

The spouse's benefit is reduced only for the spouse who is entitled because of his or her age. If the spouse has worked under Social Security and is entitled to a retirement benefit on his or her own account, see Section 302.

The reduction formula applicable to spouse's benefits is $25/36$ of 1% of $1/2$ of the worker's primary insurance amount for each of the first thirty-six months of entitlement to the spouse's benefit before full retirement age, and $5/12$ of 1% for months in excess of thirty-six months. The reduction factor goes by months, not by years, so taking a reduced benefit when you are age 62 and 11 months and taking it when you are exactly age 63 is one additional month of the reduction factor.

Example: Wanda is 63. She never worked. Her husband is entitled to a benefit with a primary insurance amount of $600.00. Wanda becomes entitled to the spouse's benefits when she is fifteen months under age 65. To figure her benefit amount, take $1/2$ of her husband's primary insurance amount ($600.00

divided by 2 equals $300.00). Find 1% of $300.00, which is $3.00, and multiply that by $\frac{25}{36}$ of $3.00, for a total of $2.08. Multiply this amount times 15 reduction months for a figure of $31.20. This is subtracted from $300.00 to result in a monthly benefit amount of $268.80, rounded down to the nearest dollar of $268.00. (see Sec. 705.6.)

If Wanda had worked and therefore had a primary insurance amount of $200.00, her benefit would be figured as follows. First we take her own primary insurance amount and reduce it by fifteen reduction months using the formula described in Section 703.1. The $200.00 is reduced because of her age to $183.30, rounded down to $183.00. Her spouse's benefit is determined and reduced. The spouse's benefit is $100.00 (the difference between $\frac{1}{2}$ of her husband's primary insurance amount and her own primary insurance amount). It is reduced fifteen months using the formula described in this section. The $100.00 is reduced to $89.50 and rounded down to $89.00. Her monthly benefit amount is composed of her own reduced benefit in the amount of $183.00 plus the reduced spouse's benefit in the amount of $89.00 for a total benefit payable of $272.00.

Instead of using this formula, another formula is used by the Social Security Administration (SSA). The formula is 144 minus the number of reduction months, times $\frac{1}{2}$ of the worker's primary insurance amount, divided by 144, rounded down to the nearest dollar, or:

$$[(144 - RM) \times \tfrac{1}{2} PIA]/144.$$

Use the difference between ½ of the spouse's PIA and your own PIA if you are eligible on your own account.

Another method of figuring the spouse's benefit is to use a reduction factor from the chart in Appendix E. Multiply ½ of the worker's primary insurance amount times the reduction factor corresponding to the number of reduction months. For example, the factor for fifteen reduction months is .895. To figure Wanda's spouse's benefit from the previous example (assuming she was not entitled to a benefit on her own account), take 300 (½ of her husband's primary insurance amount) times .895 to arrive at the reduced wife's benefit amount of $268.50, rounded down to $268.00.

NOTE: *The reduction stays in effect for all months before age 65, but then is readjusted to exclude a reduction for any month before age 65 for which no full monthly benefit is paid. (see Sec. 704.3.) If all benefits before age 65 are paid, the reduction stays in effect for life.*

The maximum amount of the reduction for age based on thirty-six reduction months is 25%.

Section 703.3 Reduction for Age: Widow(er)'s Benefits

Widow(er)s who are entitled to benefits because of age will have their benefit amounts reduced for any month before full retirement age for which they are entitled to a benefit. A disabled widow(er) under age 60 receives the same benefit amount as a widow(er) at age 60. For benefits payable before January 1984, widow(er)s who were entitled to disabled widow(er)'s benefits before age 60 have an additional reduction of $^{43}/_{240}$ of 1% for each month of entitlement before age 60. Beginning with those born in 1940 and later, additional reduction months are applied because the full retirement age has been increased above age 65. See the discussion of this at the beginning of this section. The applicable full retirement age for widow(er)s depends on the year of birth according to the following chart.

If the birth date is...	then full retirement age is...
1/2/40–1/1/41	65 years and 2 months
1/2/41–1/1/42	65 years and 4 months
1/2/42–1/1/43	65 years and 6 months
1/2/43–1/1/44	65 years and 8 months
1/2/44–1/1/45	65 years and 10 months
1/2/45–1/1/57	66 years
1/2/57–1/1/58	66 years and 2 months
1/2/58–1/1/59	66 years and 4 months
1/2/59–1/1/60	66 years and 6 months
1/2/60–1/1/61	66 years and 8 months
1/2/61–1/1/62	66 years and 10 months
1/2/62 and later	67 years

The formula specified in the Social Security Act for widow(er)'s benefits is a reduction of $^{19}\!/_{40}$ of 1% of the primary insurance amount for each month before full retirement age at the time entitlement begins. This works out to a 28½% reduction at age 60 for those born before 1940. Reduction months will increase by an additional two months for those born in 1940 and later. However, because the maximum reduction for age can never exceed 28½%, the extra monthly reduction is spread out over the period of entitlement before full retirement age. Therefore, the reduction factor for each reduction month will vary according to the applicable full retirement age of the individual. This will depend on the year of birth.

The reduction factor is based on the number of months before full retirement age, not the number of years. For instance, if you take a reduced widow's benefit exactly at age 62, the benefit will be reduced by thirty-six reduction months if she were born before 1940. If she were born in 1943, an additional six months would apply, for a total of forty-two reduction months. Because the maximum reduction cannot exceed 28½%, a different fraction is required depending on the year of attainment of full retirement age. The benefit is reduced by a fraction of the primary insurance amount for each reduction month according to Chart 3 in Appendix E.

Regardless of the amount arrived at by using a reduction formula, the widow(er)'s benefit can never be greater than the amount of the monthly benefit that the husband or wife received during the lifetime if he or she were entitled. For example, if the husband took a fully reduced benefit at exactly age 62, his primary insurance amount was reduced. The widow cannot receive more than he received even if she first becomes entitled when she is at full retirement age. Likewise, any additional credit for *delayed retirement* (see Sec. 704.5) is added to the benefit of the widow.

Example: If the husband had a primary insurance amount of $500 that was increased by 3% because of delayed retirement, the widow's benefit would be figured using $515, the increased amount.

At full retirement age, the reduction factor is readjusted to exclude any reduction for a month before full retirement age for which no full monthly benefit was actually paid. (see Sec. 704.3.) A widow(er) also receives a readjustment of the reduction factor at age 62 if benefits were taken before then. (see Sec. 704.4.)

If a widow(er) is entitled to a benefit based on his or her own account at age 62, he or she has an option to take either the reduced widow(er)'s benefit or the reduced retirement benefit on his or her own account and then switch over to the other benefit unreduced at full retirement age or earlier. (see Sec. 303.)

Section 703.4 How Taking Reduced Retirement Benefits Will Affect Other Benefits

If you take a retirement benefit reduced for age, it may have an effect on other benefits payable to you or to others. The most common example of this is the case of widow(er)'s benefits. If you take your own reduced retirement benefit and then die, the amount your widow(er) may receive cannot exceed the amount you were receiving in your lifetime, even if he or she is over full retirement at the time he or she first becomes entitled. Your widow(er) will, however, receive any cost of living adjustments that may occur after your death.

If at the time you apply for reduced retirement benefits, and you are also potentially eligible for spouse's benefits, you must apply for the reduced spouse's benefit as well, even if there are no benefits actually payable because of the husband's or wife's earnings. This provision only applies if, at the time you make your application for reduced retirement benefits, your spouse is entitled to retirement or disability benefits.

Example: Your spouse turned age 65 last year and is entitled to retirement benefits and Medicare. However, due to his earnings, no benefits are payable. You are 62 years old now and you apply for your own reduced retirement benefit. Social Security will require you to file an application for the reduced spouse's benefit if one-half of the spouse's primary insurance amount is greater than your own primary insurance amount, regardless of whether cash benefits are payable to you as a spouse (your spouse's earnings will have no effect on the payment of your own benefits).

If your spouse retires in two years, the additional spouse's benefit will be paid at the reduction rate in effect at the time you first applied for your own retirement benefits, and not based on your age at the time the benefits are first payable, until you reach full retirement age, when the reduction will be adjusted. (see Sec. 704.3 and Sec. 414.)

If you are potentially eligible for widow(er)'s benefits at the time you file for reduced retirement benefits, you do not necessarily have to apply for them. You have the option of taking one or the other benefit reduced and then switching over to the other one unreduced at full retirement age. (see Sec. 303.)

If you apply for reduced retirement benefits and you have a spouse who may be entitled on your account, the fact that your benefit is reduced for age has no bearing on determining the amount of your spouse's benefit. Your spouse's benefit will be reduced according to his or her age at the time of the first entitlement. Your primary insurance amount will be reduced for the number of months you are under full retirement age at the time of first entitlement. For the spouse, one-half of your primary insurance amount will be reduced by the number of months he or she is under full retirement age at the time he or she becomes entitled. (see Sec. 703.)

If you become entitled to disability insurance benefits, the amount of your disability benefit will be reduced by the number of months you receive a retirement benefit before receiving a disability benefit.

Example: You become disabled at age 63. No benefits are payable for the first five full months of the waiting period of your disability. (see Sec. 507.) Because you are over age 62, you may receive reduced retirement benefits during the waiting period. The amount of that benefit is reduced for your age at the time you first become eligible for the retirement benefit. If you are exactly age 63 at that time, the primary insurance amount is reduced by twenty-four months using the reduction formula described in Sec. 703.

When you become entitled to the disability benefit after your waiting period, the benefit amount will be readjusted to exclude reduction for any months for which you have not received a retirement benefit. Your disability benefit is reduced, but only by the number of retirement benefits you received before becoming eligible for the disability benefits. Other benefits payable to dependents on your account will not be affected by the fact that you take reduced retirement benefits.

Section 703.5 How Taking Reduced Widow(er)'s Benefits Will Affect Your Own Benefit

If you take a widow(er)'s benefit before full retirement age, it will not affect benefits on your own account if you were born after 1928. You may switch over at full retirement age to your own unreduced benefit, if that would yield a higher amount. (see Sec. 303.)

However, if you were not born after 1928 and take a reduced widow(er)'s benefit before age 62, it may have a permanent effect on your own retirement benefits. The dollar amount of that reduction will be deducted from your own primary insurance amount at age 65. If you take your own benefit before age 65, only one reduction will be imposed, either the regular retirement reduction (see Sec. 703), or the dollar amount of the widow(er)'s reduction caused by receipt of widow(er)'s benefits for any month before age 62, whichever is higher. (see Sec. 704.4.)

Section 703.6 **Family Maximum**

If there are dependents entitled to benefits on your account, there is a maximum amount payable to your family unit regardless of what the full payment amounts to the dependents would be individually. This is referred to as the *family maximum*. For example, in a case of a retired worker who has three children under age 18 entitled on his or her account, each child's benefit, without taking the family maximum into account, would be 50% of the worker's primary insurance amount. However, depending on the amount of the primary insurance amount, there is a maximum that can be paid to the family, regardless of the number of beneficiaries.

Once this maximum is reached, it does not matter how many additional dependents are entitled on the account because the total amount payable on the earnings record cannot exceed the family maximum. Each dependent's benefit is reduced proportionately so that the total for everyone does not exceed the family maximum. The worker's own benefit is never adjusted for this purpose.

The amount of the family maximum depends on the type of benefit you receive and the year in which you become age 62, become disabled, or die (*i.e.,* the *year of eligibility*). The family maximums are the same for retirement cases and survivor cases. There is a different family maximum applicable to disability cases.

In the case of retirement and survivor accounts, the family maximum goes on a sliding scale. The scale varies depending on the year of eligibility. *Bend points* are used in the same way that a primary insurance amount is derived from average indexed monthly earnings. (see Sec. 702.2.)

The family maximum is 150% of the primary insurance amount (PIA) up to the first bend point, plus 272% of the excess of the PIA over the first bend point up to the second bend point, plus 134% of the excess of the PIA over the second point up to the third bend point, plus 175% of the PIA in excess of the third bend point. The percentages (150%, 272%, 134%, 175%) remain the same from year to year, but the bend points will change in the same way as the bend points used to compute the primary insurance amount. (see Sec. 702.2.)

In disability cases, the family maximum is 85% of the average indexed monthly earnings (see Sec. 702.2), but not more than 150% of the primary insurance amount or less than 100% of the primary insurance amount.

Once the amount of the family maximum is determined, the dependent's benefits are reduced proportionately so that the total family benefits do not exceed the maximum. In the case of retirement and disability benefits, the worker's primary insurance amount (not the benefit amount after age reduction) is deducted from the family maximum and the balance is divided among the dependents, in a proportion according to their original benefit amounts before any age reduction, as is the case with survivor benefits.

The adjustment for the family maximum is made after any deductions. (see Sec. 705.) If a dependent is not receiving benefits because of work deductions, the adjustment is made as if that dependent were not entitled on the account.

When a person is entitled as a child on more than one account, the family maximums of both accounts are combined.

A divorced spouse's or a divorced widow(er)'s benefit is not reduced for the family maximum. Other dependents' benefits on the account are not reduced because of a divorced spouse's or widow's entitlement on that account.

SECTION 704 RECOMPUTATIONS—IN GENERAL

At the time you first apply for Social Security benefits, a primary insurance amount is computed (see Sec. 702.2) and a benefit amount determined. This may be adjusted later under certain circumstances. Adjustments to the primary insurance amount or monthly benefit will affect benefits payable beginning with the effective date of the adjustment. There are four basic types of recomputations:

- cost of living increases;

- adjustments to include earnings after you first become entitled to a benefit;

- reduction factor adjustment at age 62 and full retirement age; and,

- the delayed retirement credit, which increases your benefit if you did not receive monthly benefits after full retirement age.

Section 704.1 **Cost of Living Increase**

Each year, all Social Security benefits are increased according to the *cost of living increase* that occurred during the preceding year. This is based on inflation as reflected in the Consumer Price Index. The cost of living increase is effective beginning with the month of December. Benefits are paid in arrears (see Sec. 1003) so that the benefit increase effective with December is reflected in the monthly benefit check received in January of the following year.

The cost of living increases are shown in Appendix F. The increase is computed as a percentage of the monthly benefit amount, not the primary insurance amount.

Section 704.2 **Adjustment for Earnings after Entitlement**

As noted in Section 702.2, the primary insurance amount is based on your earnings ending with the year before the year you first become eligible (survivor cases include the year of death). For example, if you apply for benefits in 2006, your earnings through 2005 will be included in the computation. However, if you work in the year you first become entitled to benefits or later, and the earnings in the later year are greater than the lowest year's earnings in the computation of your benefit, then your primary insurance amount will be increased. If the amount of your earnings in the later year is less than the lowest year's earnings there will be no increase in your benefit. (see Sec. 702.2.)

The increase is effective with January of the year after the year of the additional earnings. If you continue working, and your annual earnings are greater than the lowest year used in the computation of your benefit, the increased benefit amount will be payable beginning with January of the following year.

SOCIAL SECURITY TIP

The adjustment for earnings after entitlement increases your primary insurance amount and accordingly will increase the benefit for anyone who is receiving benefits on your account.

The Social Security Administration will automatically readjust your benefit amount to include additional earnings if it yields a higher benefit. However, the SSA is backlogged—in fact, it runs years behind. You may request an earlier readjustment.

Section 704.3 Refiguring the Age Reduction at Full Retirement Age

If you received a benefit reduced for age (see Sec. 703), the reduction factor will be adjusted effective with the month you reach full retirement age. This adjustment will eliminate the reduction for any month before full retirement age for which you did not receive a full monthly benefit. If you received all benefits, there is no adjustment. If you received a partial benefit for a month, the reduction attributable to that month's entitlement will be eliminated because you did not receive a full monthly benefit.

This reduction factor adjustment applies to all benefits that were reduced for age and is effective beginning with the month you reach full retirement age. It cannot be figured until after the year of full retirement age, because the amount of your earnings may affect whether or not any benefits will be withheld for that year.

Example: John filed for reduced retirement benefits to be effective fifteen months under full retirement age. Accordingly, his primary insurance amount was reduced by fifteen months. After he became entitled to reduced retirement benefits, he had earnings that prevented the payment of benefits for six full months and for part of a seventh month. When he reaches full retirement age, the primary insurance amount will be reduced permanently by only eight months. The month he received partial payment is also eliminated. His benefit amount will increase accordingly. No adjustment will be made until after he files an annual report for the year he reaches full retirement age (see Sec. 902.2). When the recalculation is done, it will be retroactive to the month he reaches full retirement age.

Section 704.4 Refiguring the Age Reduction for Widow(er)s at Age 62

In addition to the reduction factor adjustment as described in Section 704.3, widow(er)s who received reduced benefits before age 62 are entitled to a readjustment of their benefit amounts at age 62 to eliminate a reduction factor for any month before age 62 for which they did not receive a full monthly benefit. The increased monthly benefit will be payable beginning with the month you turn age 62.

Example: Sally applies for widow's benefits at exactly age 60 and the widow's benefit is therefore reduced by sixty reduction months. She returns to work and has earnings that require five monthly benefits to be withheld and part of a sixth month before age 62. The reduction factor based on sixty reduction months will be used to figure benefits payable up through the month before she becomes age 62. However, beginning with the month she attains age 62, the reduction factor will be adjusted to eliminate the six months for which she did not receive a full monthly benefit before 62. If she works again between ages 62 and 65, the benefit amount will be adjusted again at age 65.

Section 704.5 **Delayed Retirement Credits**

If you continue to work after *full retirement age* and your monthly benefits are withheld because of your earnings, you will receive a credit for each month beginning with the month you reach full retirement age—but not past age 70—for which you did not receive any monthly benefit. The credit varies, depending on your year of birth, from ¼ of 1% to ⅔ of 1% for each month beginning with the month of attainment of full retirement age for which you did not receive any monthly benefit. This comes out to between 3% and 8% per year. The chart in Appendix G lists the percentages according to year of birth. The credit is payable beginning with January of the year following the year in which you did not receive the benefits. In addition to the delayed retirement credit, you may also be eligible for an adjustment because of your earnings after your first year of entitlement. (see Sec. 704.2.)

You may receive a credit for any month for which benefits were not paid because an application was not filed or you voluntarily suspended benefits to earn credits.

The delayed retirement credit will not affect the benefits of any dependents on your account, but if you die and leave a widow(er), your widow(er) will be entitled to the delayed retirement credit.

You are eligible for the credit whether or not you file at full retirement age. It will be computed when you start to receive benefits. No credit is granted for any period you are not fully insured. (see Sec. 602.)

Section 704.6 **How to Expedite Adjustments for Earnings After Entitlement**

As discussed in Section 704.2, the amount of your benefit may be increased if you have earnings after the first year you become eligible for benefits, provided that those earnings are higher than the lowest year of earnings used in the computation of your benefit amount. The increase due to earnings is payable begin- ning with January of the year following the year of the earnings.

The Social Security Administration will recompute this adjustment automatically. However, it will take many months and probably years to do it. This is because there is a lag from the time you earn the wages until the time the SSA receives the report of your earnings and then acts on it to increase your benefit. You can expedite this process by making a special request. To do this, you will need your W-2 form (or tax return for the year if you were self-employed). You must go to or write to your local district office and show them your tax return or W-2. Ask that the earnings be refigured immediately instead of waiting for the automatic readjustment. The SSA will act upon your request and refigure your benefits, although it may still take several months. Whether you ask the SSA to do it immediately or you wait until they do it automatically, the adjustment will be retroactive to the first month after the year for which you had the earnings.

SECTION 705 DEDUCTIONS—IN GENERAL

After your monthly benefit amount is calculated using the rules discussed in this chapter, the Social Security Administration may, under certain circumstances, withhold part or all of the monthly benefit. The major reasons for these deductions are discussed in the following sections.

The deductions discussed here apply to the actual benefit amount figured after taking into account any reductions for age or adding any credits for later earnings or delayed retirement. Additionally, you may elect to have income tax deductions made from your benefits. (see Sec. 1409.)

NOTE: *The family maximum discussed in Section 703.6 may also cause a reduction of the amount of the benefit payable to a dependent or survivor.*

Section 705.1 **Deductions Because of Earnings**

If your earnings in a year during which you are entitled to monthly benefits are over the limits applicable to that year, then some or all monthly benefits must be withheld. The *retirement test* (or the work test as it is sometimes called) is discussed in full in Chapter 8. Once the amount of benefits to be withheld is determined by using the *annual earnings test*, full monthly benefits for that year will be withheld beginning with the first month during which you are entitled, unless you request prorating. (see Sec. 803.1.)

Example: If based on your annual earnings and applying the work test it is determined that $5,000 of monthly benefits must be withheld and your monthly benefit amount is $600, then your monthly benefit will be withheld until the $5,000 is reached. If you are eligible beginning with January to a monthly benefit of $600, then benefits for the months of January through August will be withheld in full. This would be $4,800 worth of benefits. An additional $200 must be withheld to satisfy the $5,000; therefore, the benefit for the month of September will have the $200 deducted and only $400 will be payable to you.

If you first became entitled to benefits beginning with the month of June instead of the month of January, no monthly benefits would be payable to you at all for the year because 7 x $600 is only $4,200, which is less than the amount that must be withheld based on your annual earnings.

If you have dependents entitled on your account, the dependents' benefits will also be withheld if your earnings require. However, the earnings of a dependent will affect only that dependent's benefits and will not affect the benefits of anyone else who receives payments on the account.

Section 705.2 Deductions from Disability Benefits for Workers' Compensation or Disability Payments

If you are entitled to a disability benefit and are also entitled to workers' compensation or certain other types of disability payments (see Secs. 511–512), the combination of the Social Security benefit and workers' compensation benefit (or other disability payment that is subject to the offset provision) cannot exceed 80% of your average earnings. The way average earnings are figured for these purposes is discussed in Section 511.

The offset will also apply to any dependents who receive benefits on your account, offsetting their benefits before yours.

Example: Your average earnings were $1,000 per month. You are entitled to a $500 Social Security disability benefit. You have a child who is entitled to $250 on your account. You are also eligible for $350 per month in workers' compensation benefits. Eighty percent of your average earnings is $800, but the total of the Social Security benefits and the workers' compensation benefits is $1,100. Therefore, the $300 difference must be withheld. First the child's benefit will be withheld, then $50 of your own benefit, so that the total of the Social Security benefits and workers' compensation benefits does not exceed 80% of the average earnings.

Section 705.3 Deductions from Spouse's and Widow(er)'s Benefits Because of a Government Pension

If you receive Social Security benefits as a spouse or widow(er), the amount of your benefit is reduced if you receive a government pension based on your own earnings if the public employment in which you worked was not covered by Social Security.

This government pension offset does not apply if you were potentially eligible for entitlement to a Social Security benefit as a spouse or as a widow(er) as of January 1977 and you first became eligible to a government pension from December 1977 through November 1982 (whether or not you received it). If you were not potentially eligible to the Social Security benefit in January 1977, or you became eligible for your government pension in December of 1982 or later, 100% of your government pension is deducted from your spouse's or widow(er)'s benefit.

Because of a change in the law in 1983, if you became eligible for your government pension in July 1983 or later (whether or not you actually receive it), the offset is only ⅔ of the government pension.

These offsets apply only to spouse's or widow(er)'s benefits and do not apply to benefits on your own earnings record. The government pension offset applies only if your public employment was not covered by Social Security.

Section 705.4 **Deductions to Recover an Overpayment**

If it is determined that you have been overpaid, you may have to pay the overpayment back. If you are receiving Social Security benefits, benefits will be withheld to recover the overpayment. Overpayments are discussed in detail in Chapter 11.

In the first instance, the Social Security Administration will advise you that they will withhold your full monthly benefit until the entire amount of the overpayment has been recovered. However, you may request that less than the full monthly benefit be withheld. Generally, this request will be granted if the overpayment can be recovered within three years. For instance, you were overpaid $1,000 and are entitled to a monthly benefit in the amount of $500. The SSA will seek to recover the overpayment by withholding two months' benefits. However, you may request that only part of your monthly benefit be withheld to recover the overpayment and the SSA generally will allow you thirty-six months. Instead of having the $1,000 deducted from two full months' benefits, the sum of approximately $30 per month may be deducted from your monthly benefits to recover the $1,000. The SSA does not charge any interest on this installment method of paying back the overpayment.

Section 705.5 **Deductions for Medicare Premiums**

The medical insurance part of Medicare (Part B) requires the payment of a monthly premium. The monthly premium may be higher if you did not apply for Medicare coverage on time. (see Sec. 1203.)

If you are covered by medical insurance under Medicare, the premium will be deducted from your monthly benefits, if you are receiving them. Otherwise, you will be billed on a quarterly basis. When your benefits begin, the premium will be deducted from the monthly benefit. If you have already paid a quarterly bill, you will receive a refund at a later date.

Section 705.6 **Rounding Down**

After the Social Security Administration computes your benefit (and makes any required deduction), the resulting monthly benefit amount will be reduced to the lowest multiple of $1. Rounding down is done after all the other factors used in computing benefits have been applied, including the Medicare deduction.

The only time that rounding down is not the last step is in the case of combined benefits. (see Sec. 1004.) In that case, each benefit amount is figured separately and rounded down separately. The rounded down amounts are then combined.

EARNINGS LIMITATIONS 8

Section 801 **Earnings Test—Introduction**

All beneficiaries, except those whose benefits are based on disability or are over full retirement age, are subject to a loss of benefits if their earnings exceed certain limits. The way your earnings affect benefits is called the *earnings test*. This may also be referred to as the *work test* or the *retirement test*. They are all the same. Although disabled workers are not affected by the work test, their spouses and children who receive benefits on their accounts are subject to it. (The effect of a disabled beneficiary's earnings is discussed in Section 504.)

Section 802 **Earnings Limits—In General**

If your yearly earnings are below the annual limits, there is no effect on benefits. If your yearly earnings are over the annual limit, you lose one dollar in benefits for every two dollars over the limit, except for the year you reach full retirement age. In that year, you lose one benefit dollar for every three earned dollars over the limit. There are other advantages that apply in that year. The limits are significantly higher and only earnings for months in that year before the month you attain full retirement age are counted. Whether or not you are in the year you reach full retirement age, there is also a monthly limit rule that applies, but usually for only one year. (see Sec. 804.) The earnings limits for different years are listed in Appendix G.

The earnings of a retired worker affect all dependents receiving benefits on his or her account, with the exception of a divorced spouse. (see Sec. 204.3.) However, if the worker first becomes entitled to benefits in or after the ex-spouse's benefits, but only for two years. A dependent's earnings will not affect the worker or any other dependent on the same account. Likewise, the earnings of a person receiving survivor benefits will not affect anyone else on that account.

Only earned income is considered for these purposes. (see Sec. 805.) Income such as dividends or interest is not included (see Sec. 806.) All earnings for the year are counted—even your earnings before you become eligible for benefits or after your entitlement ends. However, for the year you reach full retirement age, only earnings before the month you reach full retirement age are counted. (See Secs. 807 and 808 for special rules.)

If you have a short taxable year, which may occur when you switch from a calendar to a fiscal year, the annual earnings limit is prorated in the same way as the year of death. (see Sec. 810.)

Section 802.1 **Earnings Limits: Under Full Retirement Age**

If you will not reach full retirement age during the year, you lose one dollar of benefits for every two dollars over the annual limit for that year. All earnings for the year are included, even those earned before your eligibility for benefits. Earnings limits are listed in Appendix G. You may receive benefits for any month your earnings are less than the monthly limit, usually for only one year. (see Sec. 804.)

To determine the amount of benefits that must be withheld, subtract the yearly limit from your annual earnings and divide the remainder by two.

Section 802.2 **Earnings Limits: Year of Attainment of Full Retirement Age**

If you reach full retirement age at any time during the year, you lose one dollar in benefits for every three dollars over the annual limit. (see Appendix G.) Only earnings for months in the year before the month you reach full retirement age are included, even those earned before your eligibility for benefits.

NOTE: *You may receive benefits for any month your earnings are less than the monthly limit (see Sec. 804), but usually you may take advantage of this for only one year.*

To determine the amount of benefits that must be withheld, subtract the yearly limit from your countable earnings, and divide the remainder by three.

Section 802.3 **Earnings Limits: After Full Retirement Age**

Beginning with the month you reach full retirement age, you can earn as much as you like and still collect all of your Social Security benefits. The earnings limits no longer apply. If you are an employee, only the amount of money you earn through the month before the month of full retirement age will count. For example, if you reach full retirement age in July, only your earnings from January 1 through June 30 are included for the work test. You should not report your earnings from July 1 on. If you are self-employed, divide your annual earnings by 12 and then multiply the answer by the number of months before the month you reach full retirement age.

SECTION 803 HOW EARNINGS ARE CHARGED AGAINST MONTHLY BENEFITS

Whenever you earn over the yearly exempt amount, the Social Security Administration will withhold the required amount (see Sec. 801) of Social Security benefits beginning with the earliest month of entitlement. Social Security will withhold full monthly benefits until the entire amount that has to be withheld for the year is withheld. (See Sec. 806 for exceptions.) They do not prorate the withholding over the course of the year unless you request to have this done. (see Sec. 803.1.) Instead, they withhold all benefits beginning with the first month of eligibility until the full required amount has been withheld.

Example: Harold is entitled to $900 a month from Social Security. He expects to have excess earnings requiring $2,000 to be withheld from his Social Security benefits. Social Security will withhold his entire checks for January and February. They will withhold $200 for March, and pay him $700 for that month. He will receive his full $900 benefit for the months of April through December. All the withholding is done before any benefits are paid to him.

If one or more dependents receive benefits on your account, any partial payment is allocated to each beneficiary proportionate to his or her share of the total family benefits.

Example: Now assume Harold has a wife Beatrice who is entitled to $450 a month on Harold's account. The $2,000 would be withheld as follows:

- January—
  - Harold, $900
  - Beatrice, $450
- February—
  - Harold, $434
  - Beatrice, $216

Both would receive full checks for March through December.

If Beatrice had excess earnings instead of Harold, only her benefits would be withheld.

A dependent's earnings will never require withholding of the worker's or another dependent's benefits. Likewise, the excess earnings of a survivor will not affect another survivor's benefits.

Excess earnings are not carried over to another year. Only the benefits payable in the year of the earnings are subject to withholding. (See Sec. 806 regarding the monthly earnings test.)

Section 803.1 **Prorating**

Although Social Security procedures usually require full withholding of benefits until all required benefits are withheld, you may request that the withholding of benefits be prorated over the course of the year. Instead of receiving no benefits for the normal withholding period and then full benefits for the remainder of the year, you may choose to receive partial benefits.

In the previous examples, the $2,000 to be withheld could be spread over twelve months, deducted from each month's benefits, instead of waiting until March to receive any benefits.

If the period for prorating does not extend into the following year, your written request for prorating will be granted. The amount payable (before Part B Medicare deductions) must be at least $25 per month. Prorating of work suspensions will not be granted if you have an existing overpayment. (see Sec. 1101.)

Prorating may be extended up to June of the following year, but only if you claim that loss of benefits will cause a financial hardship or require you to significantly revise your retirement plans, and there is no expectation of excess earnings for the next year. The Social Security Administration will ask you to explain this in writing.

SECTION 804 MONTHLY EARNINGS TEST

If your earnings for a year are over the earnings limits, the Social Security Administration (SSA) will determine the amount of benefits that must be withheld. No benefits will be withheld from a *nonservice* month, no matter how high the annual earnings may be. The way nonservice months are determined is called the *monthly earnings test*. Under this rule, you have a nonservice month for any month after entitlement in which you earn under a certain amount, if you are an employee. If you are self-employed, the test is whether you render substantial services to your business. The monthly limits for employees vary depending on your age and the year involved. Amounts are listed in Appendix G.

If you are self-employed, the dollar limits do not apply. Instead, the *substantial services* rule is used. Generally, if you spend more than forty-five hours per month at your business, your services are considered substantial. If you work fewer hours per month, the services are not substantial and you may have a nonservice month. If your business is highly remunerative, such as a lawyer, doctor, consultant, etc., more than fifteen hours per month is considered substantial.

You may be eligible for more than one nonservice month in a year, but you are not eligible for nonservice months in more than one year (with some exceptions). The year in which you are eligible for nonservice months is called a *grace year*. It is the first year in which you have a nonservice month. This is not necessarily the first year you are entitled to benefits.

Example: John turns 63 years old in 2007 and applies for benefits. Although he continues working and earns over the monthly amount in all months of 2007, some benefits are payable because the amount to be withheld based on his yearly earnings is less than the total of his benefits for the year. (see Sec. 408.) Because he has no nonservice months in 2007 this is not a grace year. He has even higher earnings in 2008, enough to require withholding of all benefits.

However, he earns under the monthly limit during the months of August and September. Because these are nonservice months, he is paid his benefits for those months despite his annual earnings. Therefore, 2008 is his grace year. He works in 2009 and again his earnings require withholding of all benefits. He has no earnings in July, August, or September, but these benefits are withheld based on his annual earnings because he has already used his grace year.

There are two situations in which certain beneficiaries are entitled to a second grace year. The first case applies to a child, a spouse with child in care (see Sec. 204.2), or a young widow(er). (see Sec. 204.7.) These beneficiaries receive a second grace year for the year in which their entitlement terminates, unless the termination is because of death or change to another type of benefit with no break in entitlement.

The second case applies to any beneficiary who receives one type of benefit that terminates, but then becomes entitled to another type of benefit with at least a one-month break entitlement. The first year with a nonservice month during which the beneficiary is entitled to the second benefit is a grace year.

SECTION 805 INCOME THAT COUNTS

Under the annual earnings test, your earnings are the sum of gross wages plus net earnings from self-employment, minus any net loss from self-employment. Wages are counted even if they are not covered by Social Security tax (FICA). Bonuses and awards are counted if they were actually earned during the year. Advances against future commissions are counted if you are an employee.

Dividends and interest received by a dealer in stocks and securities are counted if produced by inventory for resale. Profit-sharing payments from a plan that is not tax-exempt are included. Real estate dealers who hold property for resale must include rental income from such property.

Royalties received from a copyright or patent obtained in or after the year you turn age 65 are counted for deduction purposes. However, royalties received from such property obtained before the year you turn age 65 are not counted beginning with the year you turn age 65.

Sick pay received during the first six months after stopping work is included, as well as temporary disability insurance, unless you paid the premiums for it.

Travel and business expenses paid to an employee are counted, unless they are specifically identified as such at the time the payment is made. Vacation pay is counted, but if it is paid at or after the termination of employment and is attributable to a prior year, it may not be counted for the current year's earnings.

Before 1984, payments of idle-time, standby, *subject to call*, and other such payments for a nonwork period after age 62 were not counted for the work test. Beginning January 1, 1984, these types of payments became included as earnings.

SECTION 806 INCOME THAT DOES NOT COUNT

Payments that do not represent wages or self-employment income are not included for purposes of the retirement test. You do not count items such as:

- interest;

- dividends;

- capital gains;

- legal damages (unless they result from a legal action for wages);

- wages that are used to hire a substitute employee;

- payments to an established employer cafeteria benefits plan;

- rental income;

- income from a hobby, prizes, or awards;

- royalties from a work personally created on which a patent or copyright was obtained before the year you turn 65 if the royalties are received in or after the year you turn age 65;

- sick pay received more than six months from the last month you worked;

- unemployment benefits; and,

- workers' compensation benefits.

Certain self-employment income may be excluded. (see Sec. 808).

Although a particular payment may be considered wages for deduction purposes, if it is attributable to a time before your entitlement, it may not affect your benefits. (see Sec. 807.)

Section 807 When Earnings are Counted

Wages are counted as earnings for the year in which they were earned. It is presumed that wages paid in a year were earned in that year, unless you show otherwise. Self-employment income is earned when received (or accrued, for those on the accrual method), regardless of when the services were rendered.

Sometimes special payments are made at or near retirement, such as advances, back pay, bonuses, severance pay, accrued vacation pay, holiday pay, and so forth. If these payments were earned in an earlier year, they are not included in the earnings test for the year of retirement. Likewise, the month in which such a payment is earned may be important for determining nonservice months. (see Sec. 804.)

If your employment has not ended, payments for sick pay, holiday pay, and vacation pay are earned at the time of your absence. Advances against commissions, payment in lieu of vacation, and occasional bonuses are considered earned in the month of payment. If you can establish that they should be attributed to a different period, the Social Security Administration will do so. Back pay, regular bonuses, and school teacher's summer pay is considered earned in the month for which payment is made.

If the payment is made at the time of or after your employment terminates, the wages are considered earned as of the last month worked. However, if it is clear from a written plan that the payment relates to an earlier period, it will not be counted as earnings for the current period. For example, if you have accrued a month's vacation that you could have taken in an earlier year, you do not include that as earnings for the retirement test when you are paid for that vacation time upon your retirement.

The next section discusses the self-employment income exclusion.

SECTION 808 SELF-EMPLOYMENT INCOME AND LOSSES

Net losses from self-employment may be deducted from gross wages and other self-employment income for the year.

Example: Jim is a plumber who earns $10,000 in wages. He also is self-employed in a plumbing business. He has $7,000 in net losses in his business. Only $3,000 is counted as earnings for the retirement test.

For purposes of the retirement test, you may exclude all self-employment income attributable to services rendered before your first month of entitlement, but received (or accrued for those who use that method) in a year after the first year of entitlement. For example, if your first month of entitlement is December, you may exclude from the next year's earnings (for the retirement test only) that income attributable to services performed before December of your year of entitlement.

SECTION 809 SPECIAL PROBLEMS FOR BUSINESS OWNERS

As a business owner, it is easy for you to reduce your salary when you reach retirement age to qualify for benefits even if you do not actually retire. The Social Security Administration has special procedures for retirement claims from people who own a business. They will not simply accept your word that your earnings are below the earnings limit. The SSA will assume that your earnings are over the limit unless you can prove to their satisfaction that your actual services have been reduced.

If you have sold your business, they will want to see the contract and other documents to make sure it is a bona fide transaction and not merely a sham designed to make you eligible for benefits without really retiring. If you will continue in the business, they will want an explanation of why your income is reduced. Any reduction in income must correspond to a reduction in your services. Stopping or cutting your salary, without a reduction in your duties, is not sufficient. They will want to know who will assume your former duties and what qualifications they have to do it.

The SSA will require you to give a signed statement detailing the nature of your business, your pre-retirement and post-retirement duties, the names and addresses of your major customers and suppliers, how many hours you will spend at the business and on what days, and what kinds of payments you receive from the business and how much.

They will require you to submit your personal and business tax returns for the last two or three years, as well as any other records they believe are important, depending on your type of business.

They will check up on the statements you give. They will call your suppliers and customers to see if you are still personally dealing with them. A field representative may call upon your place of business posing as a customer to see if you are there and if you are working. They will scrutinize your tax returns to see if you are overstating deductions or taking money out of the business in a disguised form.

The SSA does all of this to prevent payment of retirement benefits to someone who has not really retired. If they decide that your retirement is questionable, they will not pay your benefits.

Before you file for benefits, if you are not selling or closing your business, you must be prepared to explain, in full detail, why your earnings will be less and who is taking over your duties. Expect them to confirm everything you tell them. Even if they start your checks, they may reevaluate your case in three months, six months, or a year. If they do, and then decide you were never really retired, they may claim that they overpaid you and require a refund.

A consultation with a lawyer with Social Security experience would be wise. You should do this before you go to the Social Security office. You are within your rights to intentionally restrict your earnings to qualify for benefits if you wish, but your earnings must be fairly related to your actual services.

SECTION 810 SPECIAL RULE FOR THE YEAR OF DEATH

The *full annual exempt amount* is used in the year of death. The SSA will use the full annual exempt amount for a beneficiary who dies in the year of reaching full retirement age, even if he or she died before attaining full retirement age.

SECTION 811 WORK OUTSIDE THE UNITED STATES

If you are under age 70 and work in a foreign country for forty-five hours in any one month, your benefit is suspended for that month, unless the work is covered by U.S. Social

Security tax. It does not matter how much your earnings are, even if the totals for the year or month are under the regular limits. (see Secs. 801–802.3.) Disability benefits are not subject to this rule. Benefits for any dependent on your account are also suspended, with three exceptions:

- a divorced spouse (divorced for at least two years);

- if the worker was deported; and,

- if the worker is an alien whose benefits are suspended because of the *alien nonpayment of benefits law*. This law prohibits payments, including disability benefits, to aliens who reside out of the country for more than six months.

REPORTING REQUIREMENTS 9

SECTION 901 REPORTING REQUIREMENTS— IN GENERAL

After you have become entitled to Social Security benefits, you must report any change that may affect your continued eligibility to receive benefits to the Social Security Administration. For all types of beneficiaries, earnings must be reported if they go over the earnings limits for the year, except those who receive benefits on account of disability. (see Chapter 8.) In addition to earnings, anything else that affects benefits must be reported, including marriage, remarriage, divorce, not having a young child in your care for a month, stopping school attendance, or in some cases, residing in certain foreign countries.

SECTION 902 REPORTING EARNINGS— IN GENERAL

The amount of money you are allowed to earn without any effect on your benefits depends on how old you are and which year is involved. There are special reporting requirements for disability cases. (see Sec. 908.)

If you receive benefits for another—for example, a mother who receives benefits for a child—it is your responsibility to report the earnings for that person.

Earnings can be reported to the Social Security Administration by a telephone call to the local district office or by a letter. If you have earned over the allowed amount for a year during which you have received benefits, you will be required to file an annual report of earnings. (see Sec. 902.2.)

Section 902.1 When to Report Earnings

When you file a claim for Social Security benefits, you will be asked how much you expect to earn during that year. Additionally, if you file in the last three months of a year, you will be asked to estimate how much you expect to earn in the following year. The benefits paid to you will be based upon your estimates. Likewise, when you file an annual report of earnings (see Sec. 902.2), you will be asked how much you expect to earn in the coming year, and your benefits will be based on that. If you estimate that you will earn under the exempt amount for a year, you will be paid all benefits due. If you say you will earn over the exempt amount, the Social Security Administration (SSA) will deduct the required amount from your monthly payments. (see Sec. 803.)

If you later expect that your earnings will be different from what you reported to the SSA, you should notify them immediately. If your earnings will be higher, you may be overpaid and have to pay money back. (Overpayments are discussed in full in Chapter 11.) If you will earn less, you may be delayed in receiving money due you if you do not notify them promptly.

Sometimes people report that they will not earn over the limit for the year, but then it turns out that they do. Many people think that they do not have to tell the SSA until they actually earn over the limit. This is incorrect and could result in an overpayment.

SOCIAL SECURITY TIP

Notify the SSA at the time you expect your earnings to go over the limit, not when they actually do.

Except for annual reports of earnings (see Sec. 903), there are no formal requirements for notifying the SSA of an expected change in your earnings. You may call them on the phone, write a letter, or visit the district office. If you write, address your letter to the attention of the "Service Unit" and include your claim number. (see Sec. 1407.) The letter should be mailed to your local district office. (see Sec. 105.)

There are no penalties for not notifying the SSA about a change in your earnings estimate, but you must file an annual report for the year if your earnings are over the limit. You may be overpaid and have to pay money back if you delay telling the SSA about an increase in your earnings.

Section 902.2 **Annual Report of Earnings**

Even though you are responsible for reporting your earnings if they affect payment of your benefits, the SSA may consider the earnings information on your W-2 and/or your self-employment tax return as the annual report of earnings required by law. The SSA will use that information to adjust benefits under the earnings test. This means that most people will not have to make a specific report to the SSA. However, you will need to provide additional information if the information on record is incorrect or incomplete and affects the payments of benefits. If you fail to report information that will require recovery of overpaid benefits, you may be subject to financial penalties. (see Sec. 903.)

Additionally, if one of the following situations applies, you should submit a report to the SSA because you may be entitled to additional benefits if benefits were withheld.

- You are eligible to receive benefits under the monthly earnings test.

- Some or all of the earnings reported on your W-2 were for work done in prior years and are not shown in the "Nonqualified plan" box on the W-2.

- You earned wages above the applicable exempt amount and also had a net loss in self-employment.

- You had wages reported on a W-2 that will also be reported on a self-employment tax return. (For example, if you are a minister or church worker.)

- You filed a self-employment tax return but did not perform any services in the business.

- You are self-employed and file tax returns on a fiscal year basis.

- You are a farmer, filed a self-employment return reporting earnings of more than the applicable exempt amount, and you received federal Agricultural Program payments or had income from carry-over crops.

- Your estimated earnings are over the exempt amount, and you had some benefits withheld during the year, but you had no earnings for the year.

- You request prorated or deferred work suspension. (see Sec. 803.1.)

The following information must be reported when filing an annual report of earnings:

- name, address, and claim number of the beneficiary;

- taxable year being reported;

- total wages earned in the year (regardless of amount paid);

- amount of net earnings or net loss from self-employment;

- nonservice months (if monthly test applies);

- stop work month and year (if applicable); and,

- name and address of person making the report.

If required because your tax return or W-2 information is not accurate, an annual report must be filed by you on or before April 15 of the year following the taxable year, if the taxable year ends on December 31. If you file based on a fiscal year, the report is due three months and fifteen days after the close of the fiscal year. You may report by phone, mail, or a visit to your local Social Security office.

NOTE: *If a due date falls on a Saturday, Sunday, legal holiday, or federal nonwork day, the due date is the next working day.*

Section 903 Late Filing—Penalties

If you do not file your annual report of earnings by the deadline (see Sec. 902.2), you will be subject to penalties if you were overpaid during the year in question. The amount of the penalty is equal to one month's benefit if this is the first time you failed to file the annual report on time. If this is the second time, the penalty will be equal to two months' benefits. If it is the third time or more, the penalty will be three months' benefits.

The Social Security Administration uses the benefit amount for December of the year involved for the penalty. If the amount of money overpaid for the year is less than the monthly benefit amount for the December benefit, the penalty will be equal to the amount you were overpaid. For example, if you were over-paid only $100, the penalty will be $100, instead of the monthly benefit amount (minimum of $10) but only for the first time you fail to file an annual report. For a second or later failure, the normal penalty may be less if the amount of your overpayment could have been deducted from a lesser number of months' benefits. In that case, the penalty will be equal to only the number of months that would have had deductions because of the earnings.

Example: A beneficiary with a monthly benefit rate of $400 per month has an overpayment of $600. This is the third time he has failed to file his annual report. The penalty for failure to file will be equal to only two months of benefits ($800) because the $600 overpayment would have caused deductions in only two months.

If you were paid the correct amount of benefits for the year being reported or if money is due for the year being reported, there is no penalty for filing a late report of annual earnings.

If you can establish that you had good cause for not filing in a timely manner, there will be no penalty. Generally, good cause can be found only if you took all reasonable steps to comply with your responsibility or you were prevented from filing due to circumstances beyond your control, such as a physical or mental condition.

SECTION 904 REPORTING CHANGES IN MARITAL STATUS

If you receive spouse's, widow(er)'s, or child's benefits, you must report any change in your marital status. If you become divorced from the worker, although you may be eligible to continue receiving benefits as a divorced spouse, you must report the divorce anyway. If you were married to the worker for ten years and are at least 62 years old, you may still receive benefits. (see Sec. 204.3.)

If you receive benefits as a divorced spouse or widow(er), you must report a remarriage. Divorced widow(er)s who remarry after age 60 (or after age 50 if disabled) may continue to receive benefits the same as nondivorced widow(er)s who remarry after age 60. Widow(er)'s benefits will not be terminated due to remarriage if it occurs after age 60. Nevertheless, you should report it for the record and to change your name and identification code. (see Sec. 1407.)

If a person who receives a child's benefit marries, the benefits will usually terminate. The marriage must be reported to the SSA.

If one Social Security beneficiary marries another, depending on the types of beneficiaries marrying, the benefits may not terminate even though they would if the marriage did not occur between beneficiaries. A chart is located at Appendix I that tells you whether or not benefits will terminate due to remarriage.

If you receive child's benefits as a stepchild, you do not have to report the divorce of your natural parent and your stepparent. This will not affect the stepchild's eligibility. Once the stepchild is entitled to benefits on the stepparent's account, the benefits will continue despite a divorce.

If you receive benefits only on your own account, you do not have to report any change in your marital status, unless you wish to enter your name change.

SECTION 905 REPORTING CHANGES IN STUDENT STATUS

As noted in Section 205.1 and in Section 409, a child may continue to receive child's benefits after age 18—but not past age 19—if he or she is a full-time student in elementary or secondary school. If you are receiving benefits on this basis, you must report any change in your full-time school status. If you are over age 18 and no longer a full-time student, your benefits will terminate.

SECTION 906 REPORTING CHILD NOT IN CARE

If you receive spouse's or widow(er)'s benefits because you have a child in your care (see Sec. 213), your monthly benefit will be suspended for any month you do not have the child in your care. This does not terminate your benefits; it only suspends them. (see Sec. 1008.) You must report this to the Social Security Administration (SSA). Short absences of less than one month do not count. It must be reported only if the child is gone for the entire month. If the child goes away on vacation, your benefits will not be suspended if you are still responsible for the child's upbringing and are exercising parental control and supervision. However, if the child goes to live with another parent for more than one month, you must report it because it will result in suspension of your benefits for that month.

A penalty may be imposed for failing to report not having a child in your care. The penalty amount is equal to the benefit amount for the first month of a period in which the child is not in your care. The penalty for a second failure is twice the benefit amount. The penalty for a third subsequent failure is three times the benefit amount. The penalty cannot exceed the amount of benefits that should have been suspended.

SECTION 907 **REPORTING DEATH**

The death of a Social Security beneficiary should be reported immediately. A check received after the death of a beneficiary cannot be cashed. It must be returned to the Social Security Administration.

SOCIAL SECURITY TIP

If you cash a check for a beneficiary who has died, you may be subject to criminal penalties.

A benefit is not payable for the month of death. A check received after the death may be due for an earlier month. If so, it must be reissued by the SSA. It cannot be cashed. (see Sec. 1408.)

In the case of a husband and wife who receive a combined check, it should be brought to the local Social Security district office. A service representative or a claim representative will stamp the back of the check with a special endorsement called a *superendorsement* that will make it payable to the surviving beneficiary. You can then cash the check. The SSA will adjust your future benefits to take this into account.

SECTION 908 REPORTING CHANGES IN DISABILITY CASES

People who receive benefits because they are disabled do not have to file an annual report of earnings because the annual earnings limitations do not apply in disability cases. The earnings test does apply to spouses or children of disabled workers. Any work activity by a disabled beneficiary should be reported immediately to the SSA, regardless of the amount of earnings expected to be earned. The fact that you are working may have an effect on your continued eligibility to receive disability benefits. (see Sec. 504.)

If you receive benefits because of disability, you should report any medical improvement in your condition because you may no longer be totally disabled. There is no penalty for failure to report a medical improvement.

SECTION 909 REPORTING WORK OUTSIDE THE UNITED STATES

You must report to the Social Security Administration as soon as you have worked forty-five hours or more in one month in a foreign country. (see Sec. 811.) You are subject to a penalty for failing to report in the same way as penalties are imposed for failing to report that a child is not in your care. (see Sec. 906.)

Payment, Nonpayment, and Nonreceipt of Checks 10

Section 1001 Checks—In General

Social Security benefits are issued by the Treasury Department on regular green government checks or deposited electronically directly into your bank account. The checks have the

Social Security number of the worker on whose account the benefits are based and will also have the beneficiary identification code that indicates which type of benefit is being received. (see Sec. 1407.) The checks can be mailed to your home, to your post office box, or directly to your bank. (see Sec. 1006.) They can be sent in care of someone, but the Social Security Administration (SSA) will want an explanation. They want to make sure that no one else is depriving you of your Social Security benefits. In case of extraordinary circumstances—for example, if you do not reside in a permanent dwelling or do not have a fixed home or mailing address—the local SSA office manager may permit your checks to be mailed to you care of the district office. However, fear of theft of your mail is not considered a good reason.

Social Security benefits are not assignable and are not subject to attachment or levy by creditors—except for an Internal Revenue Service (IRS) levy to collect unpaid federal taxes and garnishment to enforce child support and/or alimony obligations.

SECTION 1002 FIRST CHECK

When you apply for Social Security benefits, you may be required to submit certain documents. (see Chapter 4.) After you have submitted everything required, you should receive your first check in about one month. This is the average processing time. Sometimes it takes as little as ten or fifteen days, sometimes it can take up to three months. It is rare, but occasionally a case can take more than three months before the first check is sent out.

The check will not be paid until it is due. If you apply in advance of the time you are first eligible for benefits, you will not receive it until you have met the eligibility requirements. For instance, if you apply for retirement benefits three months before you turn age 62, you will not receive the check until you turn 62.

If you have applied for Social Security benefits after the first month in which you are entitled, the first check may include retroactive benefits due for the past period. (There is a full discussion of applications and retroactivity in Chapter 4.)

The Social Security Administration has different procedures and systems; for processing cases. Some cases can go through a computer system; other cases cannot. The cases that can go through the computer are processed much more quickly than the others. About a month after you apply for benefits, you can call the local district office to find out when you may expect to receive the first check. They usually will not be able to tell you how long it will take until approximately four weeks after you apply. They will be able to tell you at that time whether you can expect it within a few weeks or if it could take a few more months.

Section 1003 Regular Monthly Checks

After you have become entitled to Social Security benefits, you will receive your checks on a monthly basis. The checks are paid one month in arrears. This means, for example, that the check you receive in May is the benefit due for the month of April. For beneficiaries entitled before May 1997, the checks are paid on the third day of the month unless the third is a Saturday, Sunday, or a holiday, in which case it will be paid before the third.

For beneficiaries entitled beginning May 1997, the check payment days are staggered according to birthday. If your birthday is the on the first through the tenth day of the month, you receive your check on the second Wednesday of the month. For those born on the eleventh through the twentieth, the check comes on the third Wednesday. For those born on the twenty-first through the end of the month, it comes on the fourth Wednesday.

SECTION 1004 COMBINED CHECKS

If two or more people who live in the same household receive benefits on the same account, the SSA will usually combine the payments for each beneficiary into one monthly check. This will not be done for a parent and child. For example, if a husband and wife are both receiving benefits on the husband's account, they will get one monthly check that will have both of their names on it.

If the spouse had worked on his or her own record and is entitled to benefits on his or her own account, in addition to the spouse's benefits, the checks will not be combined. Each person will receive his or her own check.

SOCIAL SECURITY TIP

If you do not want your benefits combined into one check, you may request that they be issued separately.

If you receive combined payments in one check and one beneficiary dies, the surviving beneficiary can take the check to the local district office to have it made payable to him or her. The amount of benefits will be adjusted at a later time, although this may take several months.

SECTION 1005 SPECIAL CHECKS

After you are receiving your regular monthly checks, an increase may be due to you for different reasons. (see Sec. 704.) If the Social Security Administration increases your benefit amount after the time you are first entitled to the increase, you will receive the increases for each unpaid month retroactively in one check. For example, if you work after you first become eligible for Social Security benefits, your earnings may increase your benefit amount. (see Sec. 704.2.)

The SSA will automatically recompute your benefit, but it may take them years to do it. If you have earnings in a year after the year you become eligible for benefits, your new earnings may cause an increase in your benefit amount beginning with January of the first year after the year of the new earnings. You may request a recalculation as soon as you get your W-2 or you may wait for them to do it automatically.

Sometimes it may take the SSA years to make the recalculation, but when they do, they will pay the past-due increases in a lump sum. This check will be in an odd amount and can arrive at any time during the month, or the money can be combined with a regular check. You will usually receive a letter explaining why you are receiving the check or the odd payment, but the letter may come after you receive the check. The letter should come within about two weeks either before or after you receive the check. If you receive an odd check and you do not have an explanation letter within two weeks, contact your district office.

Section 1006 **Direct Deposit**

If you wish, you can have your Social Security checks sent directly to your bank to be deposited into your account instead of to your home. This can be very convenient for obvious reasons. You must be receiving regular monthly checks. To arrange for this, you must contact your bank; do not contact the district office. The bank will fill out the appropriate forms and it will notify the SSA. It may take up to three months. If it does not start within that time, get a copy of the form from the bank and bring it to the district office. They can make the computer inputs from the copy.

Section 1007 **Nonpayment—In General**

Regular monthly checks will stop if the SSA determines that your eligibility has terminated (see Sec. 1009) or that you are subject to suspension. (see Sec. 1008.) Before the benefits actually stop, you should receive notice of the SSA's intention to terminate or suspend your benefits. You generally have a right to appeal these decisions. (see Chapter 13.)

Sometimes you may receive only a partial benefit for the month. If you must pay back money because you have been overpaid, you may arrange for deductions from your monthly benefits over a period of time instead of withholding the full benefit amount until the overpayment is recovered.

If you are due a check for a month but you do not receive it, you should follow the guidelines in Section 1011.

SECTION 1008 SUSPENSION OF BENEFITS

In some cases, even though you remain legally entitled to benefits, the payment may be suspended. The most common example of this is where benefits are suspended because of earnings. (see Chapter 8.)

If you are a spouse with child in care or a mother/father with child in care (eligibility for these benefits is based on having a child in your care), you are subject to a suspension of benefits for any full month you do not have a child in your care. Temporary absences do not count. If your child is away on vacation with relatives or at a boarding school, you are considered to have a child in your care if you are exercising parental control and responsibility over the child. If you are separated from the other parent, you are subject to suspension for any month the child is with that parent. The Social Security Administration looks at the calendar months involved and not the total number of days. If the child is in your care for at least one day during a calendar month, the benefit will not be suspended.

Another common reason for suspension of benefits is in the case of a spouse or a widow(er) who is eligible for a governmental pension based on his or her own earnings. (see Sec. 705.3.) Only two-thirds of the governmental pension offsets Social Security benefits.

If your benefits are in suspense, you are still legally entitled, although you will not receive the benefit for any suspense month. Once the event causing suspense stops, your benefits can be resumed without the need for another application. You should notify the SSA of the change and the benefits will be started again.

SECTION 1009 TERMINATION OF BENEFITS

In Chapter 2, each type of Social Security benefit is specifically described, including the events that will terminate benefits. Benefits terminate upon death, and sometimes will terminate upon divorce or marriage. Disability benefits may terminate if there is a medical recovery or you return to work.

Whatever the cause, benefits terminate the month before the month of the occurrence of the terminating event. For instance, in the case of death, if a beneficiary dies in the month of August, the benefits terminate with the month of July. This sounds strange, but it really is not. Checks are paid in arrears, so that the payment received in August is actually the payment for July. In all cases except disability (see Sec. 513), the benefit is payable for the month of termination so that although the benefits terminate the month before the month of the event, the check is payable for the terminating month. In the case of the beneficiary who dies in August, the August 3rd check, which is payable for the month of July, is due and payable. The September 3rd check, which would otherwise be due for the month of August, is not payable and must be returned.

These rules apply to all types of events causing termination of benefits, including death, marriage, remarriage, etc. Disability benefits may stop because you have returned to work or because you have made a medical recovery. In these cases, the termination of benefits occurs two months after the month the disability ceases. For example, if your disability ceases because of a medical improvement in June, the termination applies to the month of August. Benefits are payable for the month of June, July, and August, but not after August because that is the month of termination.

If you appeal a decision to terminate your disability benefits, you may request your benefits to continue until you receive a hearing. (see Sec. 1305.) If you have had a hearing but your case is still under appeal, it must be reevaluated. If you lose after the hearing, the benefits will be considered an overpayment. However, if you made the request in good faith, you may qualify for waiver. (see Chapter 11.)

SECTION 1010 LOST OR STOLEN CHECKS

If your monthly check has been lost or stolen, you should report this immediately to the Social Security Administration. They will issue a stop payment on that check and will reissue a replacement check. Usually you will receive the replacement check within fifteen days. If you find the lost or stolen check before the replacement check is issued (usually within a week or two after you reported it), you can cash the check, but you must notify the SSA that you found it. When the SSA puts a stop payment on a check, it takes a long time for it to become effective. If you receive the replacement check anyway, it must be returned.

A replacement check will have your Social Security claim number on it and will say that it is a substitute check. It will be dated as of the date it is actually issued, not the regular payment date.

If the check is not lost or stolen but is only misplaced, the SSA will not make an immediate reissue. They will wait three days after it was issued. Action is taken to immediately replace a lost or stolen check. If your check is stolen or lost, you must be able to give some reason why you believe it is stolen or lost, instead of simply misplaced.

SECTION 1011 WHAT TO DO IF YOUR CHECK DOES NOT COME

The overwhelming majority of the beneficiaries receive their Social Security checks on time each month without experiencing any delays or interruptions, but sometimes there are problems. Each month there are thousands of people across the country who do not receive their checks when due.

As noted in Section 1002, the first check after you apply for benefits can take anywhere from two weeks to three months —and sometimes more. If you do not receive the first check within a month of the time it is due, you should call your Social Security office to find out when you can expect it. Some cases can be processed through the computer system and other cases cannot. The cases that go through the computer system are done faster. If your case is not being handled this way, the SSA will tell you. Expect an additional two or three months for your check to come. If the SSA tells you that the check will come within two months, do not call them back the next week and ask where it is. Sometimes you can actually delay the processing of your claim by making too many inquiries. If you have not received your first check within ninety (90) days from the time you gave all the information and documents they requested, you have a right to an expedited payment. (see Sec. 1013.)

After your initial claim is processed, your case will be set up on the computer system so that you will receive regular monthly checks automatically. Checks are usually paid on the third day of the month. (If your check is received, but is lost or stolen, notify Social Security immediately.) If your check is not received at all, you should wait three mailing days before notifying the SSA. Sometimes delays occur with the post office.

If your regular check does not come when it should, there is no point notifying the SSA before three mailing days have passed. First of all, the Social Security telephone lines and the district office will be jammed with other people who have not received their checks on time. It will take you a long time to get through to somebody in the beginning of the month for this reason. But the most important reason for not notifying the SSA until three mailing days have passed is because the SSA will not do anything anyway. Their procedures require them to wait three mailing days before taking any action to replace the current month's check. If you should finally get through to a district office before the third mailing day after the check is due, it will simply send you a form to complete and mail back.

If you have not received the check by the third mailing day after it was due, steps will be taken to issue a replacement. If your check does not come on the third, do not get upset. In most cases you will receive it within three mailing days. If you do not receive it after that, you should notify the SSA of the nonreceipt of the check. You can visit the district office in person, call, or write a letter. The easiest way is to write a letter, because the phones and offices will be very busy in the first week of any given month. If you need to call, you may call the national toll-free line, 800-772-1213, but be prepared to wait.

If you write a letter, you should include certain basic information. Give your complete name, your correct mailing address, and your former mailing address if you have had a recent change. You must also indicate the claim number and your beneficiary identification code. (see Sec. 1407.) Your notice of nonreceipt of a check should identify which monthly check has not been received. You can do this by indicating the day the check was due, such as the September 3rd check, or you can describe it as the month for which the check is payable. For instance, the September 3rd check is payable for the August benefit. To avoid confusion, you should indicate the month for which the benefit is payable as well as the date you expected the payment. For example, you should say that it is the September 3rd check for the August benefit.

If your checks are directly deposited to your bank account, do not contact the SSA at all. The bank must send paperwork to notify the SSA. If you contact them instead of the bank, they will tell you to contact the bank because a bank officer must sign the form before the SSA can do anything.

When you mail a notice of nonreceipt of a check, address it to your local district office, attention "Service Unit." The service unit in the district office handles nonreceipt notice.

After you have sent your notice of nonreceipt, give the SSA about a week and then call to see if your notice was received. It will be easier at that time to get through to the district office and they should be able to tell you whether or not they have your notice. It takes about fifteen days after the notice of nonreceipt is processed by the district office for a replacement check to be issued. If you have not received it within fifteen days, you should again contact the district office. They will tell you when to expect the check. It is important not to call them before the time frames they give you. If you call too soon, the case may have to be pulled out of its normal processing to answer your question. This can result in even further delay.

If you have not received a regular monthly check within a month and a half after it was due, you have a right to an expedited payment. (see Sec. 1013.)

SECTION 1012 REPLACEMENT CHECKS

If you notify the Social Security Administration that your check is lost or stolen or that you did not receive it, you will be sent a replacement check. This will be a special check that may arrive at any time of the month and may be dated as of any date. You cannot keep both your regular check and the replacement check. One or the other must be returned if you should receive both. It does not matter which one is returned. You can cash whichever one you receive first. If you keep both checks, you will be overpaid and will be required to make a refund. In these cases you are almost never eligible for waiver of repayment.

Section 1013 Expedited Payments

The Social Security Act puts certain deadlines on the time when checks must be paid to you by the Social Security Administration. The rules are different depending on whether it is your first check or a regular monthly payment.

First Check

In a case involving your first check after you apply for benefits, you may request an expedited payment if the check has not been paid to you within ninety (90) days after the time you gave all the evidence that was requested by the SSA to support the claim (except in disability cases). The SSA is then required by law to pay you within fifteen days of your request.

To file the request you should go to your district office and tell them you want the expedited payment. If preferred, you may send a letter. The request must be in writing—you cannot do it over the phone. If you go to the district office, they will prepare a written request for you. If you file your request before the ninety days, the SSA will not act on it until the end of the ninety-day period.

If you have filed your application for benefits before the month you are entitled to payment, the ninety days runs from the date on which the first payment is due, not from the date you submitted your last evidence. For example, if you file in June for benefits beginning with the month of September, the ninety-day period begins running from October 3rd. (October 3rd is the payment check for the September benefits.)

Regular Monthly Checks

If you are receiving regular monthly benefits, a request for expedited payment may be filed thirty days after the fifteenth day of the month in which the payment was due. For example, if you are receiving regular monthly benefits on the third of each month, and you do not receive the check due on September 3rd, you may request an expedited payment if you have not received it within thirty days after September 15th. The payment must then be issued to you within fifteen days of that request. The request for expedited payment can be filed earlier, but it will not be acted upon until after the thirty days runs out.

If you do not receive your check despite your request for expedited payment and you are not satisfied with the explanations you are getting from the SSA, you may wish to contact an elected official. (see Sec. 1014.)

SECTION 1014 WHEN TO GO TO YOUR CONGRESSPERSON

Sometimes, even with the best efforts of the Social Security Administration's employees, problems can occur that delay payments. If you have followed the procedures outlined in the previous sections, but still have not received your check, an elected official will help push your case. You should contact your U.S. congressperson or your U.S. senator. Each congressperson's office usually has a person who keeps in touch with the Social Security Administration.

When the district office receives an inquiry from a congressperson, it will take steps to make sure that your case is handled as quickly as possible. The district office will locate your folder and put a special flag on it to indicate that there is a congressional inquiry. This will make sure that the case does not get lost in the shuffle and regular reports will be made to the manager of the district office who in turn will make reports to the congressperson's office.

It is important to contact your congressperson only when all else fails. If you contact your congressperson too soon, it may result in additional delays on your case. This is because the case may have to be pulled out of its normal processing to answer the congressperson's inquiry. Call your congressperson only after you have followed the guidelines in the previous sections.

OVERPAYMENTS 11

SECTION 1101 OVERPAYMENTS—IN GENERAL

An *overpayment* arises when you get more Social Security benefits than you are legally entitled to receive. Each year thousands of people are overpaid benefits. Overpayments occur for many reasons. Sometimes it is the Social Security Administration's fault, sometimes it is the beneficiary's fault, and sometimes it is a combination of both. Of course, the SSA would like to recover any benefits that were erroneously paid. However, the law and the Social Security rules allow for *waiver* of repayment of the overpayment. In certain cases, a beneficiary who has been overpaid will not be required to make a refund. This chapter discusses the rules and guidelines the SSA uses when determining whether or not to require a full refund of an overpayment.

SECTION 1102 COMMON CAUSES OF OVERPAYMENT

There are two separate categories of overpayments. The most typical one is called a *deduction overpayment*. In these cases the beneficiary is legally entitled to benefits, but for some other reason, part or all of the benefits should not have been paid. This situation frequently arises when the beneficiary has earnings over the limit for the year, but benefits were paid based on a lower estimate.

Another common cause of overpayments is when a new beneficiary becomes entitled on the same Social Security account. For example, a man dies and leaves his wife and two children. They become entitled to benefits. Several months later, a child by a previous marriage applies for benefits on that account. Because of the family maximum provisions (see Sec. 703.6), an overpayment arises retroactively.

When there are three or more beneficiaries receiving survivor benefits, the family maximum is usually met. When the widow and first two children filed and started receiving benefits, they were paid on the assumption that there would be only three beneficiaries on the account. When a child by a first marriage applies, his or her application can be retroactive for up to six months. Although the benefits will be refigured for the future and the first two children and widow will receive less, the benefits for the past were higher than they should have been.

Another common type of overpayment is called an *entitlement overpayment*. This occurs when you file for benefits and the SSA pays them but later discovers that you were never eligible. Any benefits you received were an overpayment.

Sometimes overpayments can occur because of clerical errors. When your benefits are being calculated, they are based on the amount of the earnings. Sometimes a clerical error can occur so that the amount of your earnings is figured at a higher level than it actually was. This means that the amount of your benefit was greater than it should have been and the difference is an overpayment.

SECTION 1103 OVERPAYMENT PROCEDURES

Once the SSA determines that a person has been overpaid, a decision must be made whether to collect back the overpayment or to waive it. If waived, the SSA will not require repayment. (The Social Security Administration's guidelines and procedures for waiver of repayment are discussed in Secs. 1104–1109.)

If the SSA requires a refund, this can be done in different ways. It may accept a partial refund as a compromise in full settlement (see Secs. 1110–1111) or allow for repayment over a period of time. (see Secs. 1113–1114.)

When the SSA determines that you have been overpaid, a letter will be sent to you advising you of that fact and the amount of the overpayment. The letter will explain how the overpayment occurred. The SSA will always request a full refund of the overpaid amount. If you disagree that there has been an overpayment or with the amount of the overpayment, you may request a reconsideration. (see Chapter 13.)

In the overpayment letter, the SSA says that it will start withholding 100% of your monthly benefits until the full amount of overpayment has been recovered. If you request an appeal, a waiver, or some other method of repayment, the SSA will hold up any further processing of the recovery until a decision has been made on your request.

SECTION 1104 WAIVER OF OVERPAYMENT

The Social Security Administration will not require you to refund an overpayment if certain conditions are met. To be eligible you must be *without fault* in causing the overpayment (see Sec. 1105) *and* repayment would either be *against equity and good conscience* (see Sec. 1106) or it would *defeat the purpose of Title II of the Social Security Act*. (see Sec. 1107.)

You must satisfy the *without fault* requirement in all cases and either one of the two alternative requirements. An overpayment may be waived if you are without fault and recovery would be against equity and good conscience or you are without fault and recovery would defeat the purpose of Title II.

Against equity and good conscience means that it would be unfair under the circumstance of your case. *Defeat the purpose of Title II* means you would lose a minimum income required by reason of retirement, death, or disability. This requirement may be met if recovery would prevent you from meeting your ordinary and necessary living expenses and you have insufficient assets.

If you are found eligible for waiver, you will not be required to repay the overpayment. The slate will be wiped clean and you will have no obligation for repayment at any time.

If you are not eligible for waiver, you will be required to repay. This can be done by a compromise settlement in a lesser sum (see Secs. 1110–1111), by partial payments (see Sec. 1114), or by deductions from your checks. (see Sec. 1113.)

SECTION 1105 **WITHOUT FAULT**

Generally, *without fault* means that you gave all information to the Social Security Administration that was necessary to determine your benefits and that you could not reasonably be expected to know that an overpayment would occur by accepting and cashing a particular check. If you cannot establish that you were without fault in causing an overpayment, the recovery of the overpayment can never be waived. *Without fault* is a requirement that must be met in all cases of waiver.

SOCIAL SECURITY TIP

The SSA may have been at fault in causing the overpayment. Nevertheless, you must establish that you were without fault. The SSA's fault does not excuse yours.

Each particular case will be examined to determine its own specific facts. The general principles are that you must report everything that may affect payment of benefits and you must exercise a high degree of care when determining whether or not a check is payable.

There are many situations that have occurred repeatedly involving the question of whether or not a beneficiary was at fault in causing an overpayment. The SSA has identified certain situations in which it is presumed that the beneficiary was without fault in the absence of information indicating otherwise.

There are some situations in which the SSA presumes the beneficiary was at fault. The most obvious case is when duplicate payments have been made. If you cash your regular monthly check and a replacement check, you will not be considered without fault. If you file an application for benefits but you are already receiving on another account, you are at fault if you accept benefits from both accounts, unless you told the SSA that you were already entitled on the first account.

You are at fault in causing an overpayment if you do not exercise a high degree of care about your monthly benefits. If, for example, you return to work but do not report this, you will be at fault if an overpayment results.

If you do not deal in good faith, you will not be held to be without fault. For example, if you incurred an overpayment in one year because of work, requested and obtained a waiver of repayment, but then worked again in the following year, you will not be considered without fault for the second year because you knew that your earnings would affect your benefits.

If you withhold information from the SSA that could affect your benefits, you will not be without fault. At the time you filed your application, you are given a receipt that lists the things that must be reported. From time to time, the SSA puts *stuffers* into check envelopes to remind you of things to report.

Examples of Without Fault

Over the years, the SSA has become aware of certain typical situations in which the overpaid person is without fault. They have identified these situations and will assume that if your case fits within these facts, you are without fault in causing the overpayment. This assumption may be overcome by other facts that show bad faith or failure to exercise a high degree of care about your monthly benefits.

Situation One

A person is usually found to be without fault if there is a mistake about the benefit rates. The SSA will not require you to know the exact amount of your monthly benefits. However, if the error is so grossly disproportionate to what your payment should be, you may be at fault.

Example: John applied for retirement benefits and was told
he would receive $900 per month. The first check
was $900, but the second check was $6,000. This
payment is so out of line with what he should have
expected that he may be at fault, unless he
attempted to verify it with the SSA. On the other
hand, if he received checks in the amount of $950
all along after he retired and then was advised a year
later that the correct amount should have been only
$900, the SSA will consider him to be without fault
in causing the overpayment because he cannot be
expected to calculate the exact benefit amount.

Situation Two

If you file for monthly benefits and you are told that you have
earned enough to be eligible but it later turns out you did not,
you will be considered without fault in causing any overpayment (unless your earnings record was fraudulent).

Situation Three

If you believed that only the net amount of your paycheck
counted toward the retirement test, you may be without
fault in causing an overpayment. If your earnings for a year
are over a certain level, it will cause a reduction in your
benefits. The gross amount (before taxes are deducted) of
earnings is what counts. Many times a beneficiary believes
that only take-home pay is counted for the annual earnings
limitation or the monthly limit. Your take-home pay is the
amount of your paycheck after all deductions, such as
income tax, union dues, insurance, hospitalization, etc. If

your net cash earnings (take-home pay) for the year are below the annual earnings limit, then the SSA will generally consider you to be without fault if you believed that only your take-home pay counted. If your net cash earnings are over the limit for the year, the SSA will consider whether or not you reported the net amount or the gross amount for purposes of the annual earnings limitations. If you report the amount of take-home pay to the SSA, this will indicate that you understood that only the take-home pay counted and not the gross pay.

SOCIAL SECURITY TIP

The Social Security Administration will want to look at your pay stubs to determine the net amount of your take-home pay. If you cannot obtain them, it will usually contact your employer to find this out.

Situation Four

You will be considered to be without fault in causing an over-payment if you relied on incorrect information from an *official source*. An official source means the SSA or another government agency that you reasonably thought was connected with the administration of Social Security, such as the Railroad Retirement Board. Misunderstanding of correctly given information does not count as misinformation for these purposes.

If you claim misinformation was given to you, the Social Security Administration will question you very closely to determine whether or not you misunderstood correct information or whether misinformation was in fact given. They will look to determine your normal understanding, because some people can understand technical requirements better than others. You must give a full explanation of your reliance on wrong information. They will ask for an explanation for your own words. The explanation will have to show what information was received; the time and place it was received; the identity, if possible, of the person who gave the incorrect information; and any and all other facts about it.

The SSA will seek to verify the statements you give by contacting people within the district office or elsewhere who you say gave you the misinformation. If supporting evidence cannot be obtained, the manager or supervisor in the office will make a report as to the likelihood of misinformation being given. If records are no longer available and there is no way to verify your allegations, they will resolve the doubt about it in your favor.

Situation Five

Sometimes a person is overpaid because he or she has earned over the allowable earnings limit for a particular year without realizing that the earnings before becoming entitled to benefits in that year would count. For example, you start receiving benefits in June. Your earnings for June through December are only $8,000, well below the annual earnings limit. But you also worked from January through May and earned $10,000. The total yearly earnings are $18,000 and will cause deductions for any month you earned over the monthly limit. (see Sec. 804.) If you received all your monthly benefits and earned over the monthly limit in all months, you are overpaid. If you believed that your earnings before you became entitled to benefits did not count for the earnings test, the SSA will consider you to be without fault in causing the overpayment.

For this rule to apply, your earnings for the year beginning with the time you become eligible must not exceed the annual earnings limit for that year. The intent of this rule is to provide for a *without fault* finding if you restrict your earnings to the yearly limit beginning with the time you become eligible for benefits. Although all your earnings for the year are included for purposes of the work test, if you were unaware of this and believed in good faith that only your earnings after entitlement counted, the SSA may find you to be without fault.

If you are an employee and your wages in the deduction months (months that are subject to withholding because of earnings) did not exceed the total monthly benefit for that month, recovery of the overpayment is deemed inequitable. In this situation, the overpayment may be waived without considering your financial circumstances.

Example: William, age 63, began his entitlement to retirement benefits in March 2007. His monthly amount was established at $900. He earned $4,000 in the months of January and February. His wife also became entitled to wife's benefits in the amount of $450. Benefit checks were issued to Mr. Smith and his wife each month beginning with March 2007 based on his statement that he would not earn over the yearly amount permitted under the law. Mr. Smith's employer later reported wages of $16,000 in 2007. It seems that Mr. Smith misunderstood the retirement test. Mr. Smith believed that he could earn the annual limit after qualifying for benefits and reduced his hours of work so his earnings would not exceed $12,960, the annual limit in 2007 for those under full retirement age ($1,296 a month for ten months). On the basis of his earnings, he and his wife were overpaid. Mr. Smith is without fault in incurring the overpayment and recovery is deemed to be against equity and good conscience because the earnings in each of the months affected by the potential deductions (March and April) are less than his monthly benefit amount for those months.

The term *eligibility* for benefits is used broadly for purposes of this rule. It does not necessarily mean legal entitlement. It will usually mean what the beneficiary understands. If the beneficiary believes that his or her earnings before filing the application do not count, the SSA will look at it from that view. If he or she believes that earnings before reaching retirement age will not count, they will apply the rule that way.

Situation Six

If your earnings for a year go over what you expected them to be, you may be found to be without fault in causing a resulting overpayment. The reason the earnings are greater must be one of the following.

- You received a retroactive increase in pay.

- Your rate of pay was higher than you realized.

- You made an agreement with your employer that your earnings would be kept below a certain limit but the employer did not restrict the earnings and you were unable to keep accurate records.

- There were five paydays in a month and you only expected four paydays (if your monthly earnings with only four paydays would be under the monthly limit), or you figured your annual earnings based on four paydays per month and you would have been under the yearly limit on that basis.

Situation Seven

You may be without fault in causing an overpayment if the SSA continued to send checks after you notified them that you returned to work or about something else that should have caused a deduction. You qualify under this rule if you believe in good faith that you are entitled to receive the checks because the SSA is still sending them to you. The SSA will want to know how and when you gave notice of the events that were reported and what your reaction was to the continued payment of monthly checks.

Many times a person will say that notice of the deduction event (such as return to work or not having a child in your care) was to be given by a relative or friend. If this is the case, the SSA will not consider you without fault because you have the duty to report these events, not someone else. However, if you routinely rely on this other person to report these things for you, the SSA may take that as a circumstance to consider.

For instance, if you are housebound or unable to speak English, and your daughter or son takes care of your affairs, the SSA may allow that as a reasonable excuse.

Situation Eight

Sometimes overpayments occur because employees receive special types of payments that they do not realize are included in annual earnings for purposes of the retirement test. If you believe in good faith that a bonus, vacation pay, traveling expense, or other similar payment was not to be included in figuring your earnings, the SSA may consider you to be without fault in causing an overpayment that was caused by the inclusion of those payments. The Social Security Administration will contact your employer to determine the amount and the type of special payment involved.

NOTE: *You must still satisfy the second part of the waiver test. (see Sec. 1104.)*

Situation Nine

Another common situation causing overpayments is when the beneficiary is confused with regard to how the annual earnings test works. An overpaid beneficiary sometimes believes that earnings over the limit for the taxable year cause deductions from your checks only for months beginning with the first month in which your earnings go over. If you promptly report to the SSA that your earnings reached that level when they did, you may be eligible for a waiver if you are overpaid. Two important factors are considered:

1. if you did, in fact, notify the SSA when your earnings reached the yearly amount or immediately thereafter and

2. if so, the waiver can apply only for months before the time you reported your earnings.

You know your earnings after you go over the limit will affect your benefit, so you cannot be without fault if you accept them.

Situation Ten

If you receive benefits as a dependent on the account of a retired worker, your benefits may be subject to deductions if the worker earns over the annual limit. (see Sec. 801.) If you were overpaid as a result, you may be without fault if you did not know (and had no reason to know) that the worker's earnings would go over the limit and you were not living with the worker. You must still meet the second part of the waiver rules. (see Sec. 1104.)

Situation Eleven

If your benefits end during a year, your earnings after termination nevertheless are counted for the work test. This may result in overpayment of benefits paid. If you believed that your earnings after termination of entitlement would not cause deductions for the earlier months, you may be without fault in causing the overpayment. You must still meet the second part of the waiver rules. (see Sec. 1104.)

The Social Security Administration will require a breakdown of your earnings to see if you earned over the yearly limit during the time you were entitled. They will require evidence of the earnings, such as pay stubs or a letter from your employer.

Situation Twelve

You may be without fault in causing an overpayment if you made a good faith effort to restrict your earnings, but you misunderstood the retirement test, or there were some other unusual circumstance. Some situations that fall under this include the following:

- a self-employed person believing the monthly wage limits applied instead of the *substantial services* rule (see Sec. 804.);

- you wanted to restrict your earnings and kept an ongoing record, but you made an arithmetical error or lost a pay slip; or,

- you believed you could earn up to the yearly limit beginning with the month of your first check until the end of the year.

The SSA will require verification of what you say, such as evidence of your wages for specific periods.

NOTE: *Without fault under this category can be found only in cases where the circumstances of the overpayment are not covered by any of the other without fault situations. If you allege without fault under one of the other situations, but you do not meet those requirements, this section cannot be used to circumvent the intent of the other provision.*

SECTION 1106 AGAINST EQUITY AND GOOD CONSCIENCE

One of the alternatives to the second part of the waiver rules (see Sec. 1104) is that recovery of the overpayment (making you pay it back) would be *against equity and good conscience*. This occurs if, relying on payment of benefits, you gave up a valuable right or changed your position for the worse. If you claim waiver because of this, the SSA will require you to give a full explanation of the circumstances. They will require verification of what you say. The evidence required will depend on the facts of your particular case.

In all cases you must establish *without fault*. (see Sec. 1105.) If you cannot establish *against equity and good conscience*, you may still be eligible for waiver if you can establish that recovery would *defeat the purpose of Title II*. (see Sec. 1107.) If you can establish *against equity and good conscience*, you do not have to prove the financial requirements necessary for *defeat the purpose of Title II*.

Whether your case will be considered to meet the requirement depends on the particular facts of the situation. The following two examples describe situations in which the requirements were satisfied.

Example 1: John applied for retirement benefits and was awarded. He resigned from his job, relying on the monthly benefits. Three years later it is discovered that his earnings record was wrong, without fault on John's part. He does not have the required insured status (see Sec. 601) and, therefore, he has been overpaid. Because of his age, he cannot get another job. Recovery of the overpayment would be against equity and good conscience.

Example 2: Agnes is a widow who applies for and receives survivor benefits. Counting on this income, she enters her daughter in college, which would not otherwise be possible. It turns out that her husband did not work long enough and Agnes is therefore overpaid. Recovery of the overpayment would be inequitable.

In certain situations you are considered to be without fault in causing an overpayment. In some of these same cases, recovery is also considered to be against equity and good conscience and you are therefore eligible for waiver of the overpayment. If so, you do not have to establish financial hardship.

Certain without fault situations are described in Sec. 1105. Situations three, four, and five of that section are also considered to meet the *against equity* rule.

SECTION 1107 DEFEAT THE PURPOSE OF TITLE II

An alternative requirement of the second part of the waiver rules (see Sec. 1104) is that recovery of overpayment would *defeat the purpose of Title II of the Social Security Act*. This is the law that provides for Social Security benefits. Its purpose is to keep the disabled, the retired, and survivors out of destitution. You meet the *defeat the purpose* requirement if recovery of the overpayment would deprive you of funds necessary for your support.

NOTE: *If you have any part of the overpaid funds in your posses-sion or under your control, you cannot establish **defeat the purpose** as to the extent of such funds, even if you purchased assets with the funds, as long as they are clearly identifiable.*

The Social Security Administration looks first at your income (from all sources) and your ordinary and necessary living expenses. (see Sec. 1109.) If you do not need all your income, then the SSA will look at your assets. If they are below certain levels, you will not have to repay the overpay-ment. (see Sec. 1108.)

If you do not meet the *defeat the purpose* requirement, you may be eligible for waiver if recovery would be against equity and good conscience. (see Sec. 1106.) In all cases, you must also be without fault for waiver to be approved. (see Sec. 1105.)

The following examples describe situations in which the requirement is and is not met.

Example 1: Virginia was overpaid $900. She had income of $195 from a private pension and $430 in Social Security benefits. She lives alone and has no dependents. Virginia listed current monthly expenses of $620, which included $275 rent for her apartment, $20 for clothes, $200 for food, $30 for medical care and prescriptions, $10 for church contributions, $30 for utilities, and $55 for auto maintenance and insurance. She submitted bills verifying her rent, utilities, prescriptions, and automobile insurance. Since the overall expenses

251

seem reasonable and necessary for ordinary living expenses, a finding of *defeat the purpose of Title II* would be justified.

Example 2: Dan was overpaid $350. He and his wife live in a small home valued at $50,000. They also own a motor boat valued at $7,000 and on which they still owe $4,000. Their only income is Social Security benefits of $600. They only have $200 in a savings account.

They state that their monthly expenses are $640 including $100 for property taxes, $300 for food, $20 for clothing, $20 for prescriptions, $50 for utilities, $50 for insurance and upkeep of their car, and $100 to repay the loan and to maintain their boat. As the boat is not a necessity and their expenses for ordinary living costs do not approach their income, a finding of *defeat the purpose of Title II* would not be justified.

Example 3: Will, his wife Mae, and son Joe, have $500 in the bank. Will lives in a low-income housing project and alleges that his total monthly expenses are only $400, consisting of rent of $80, food of $300, and telephone of $20. His income is only $380. His expenses can be presumed to be reasonable. A finding of *defeat the purpose of Title II* is justified. If, however, his monthly income were $450, *defeat the purpose of Title II* would not be justified.

Example 4: Joe was overpaid $600 because it was determined that he did not have enough work to collect Social Security benefits. He has no monthly income. He does have $5,000 in the bank. He has outstanding medical bills of $2,200 and more medical bills are coming in monthly. The medical bills will soon wipe out his assets. In this case, even though his assets exceed the limit, a decision that recovery of the overpayment would *defeat the purpose of Title II* would be justified.

Example 5: Charlie and Maureen were overpaid $1,600. They have $5,900 in a savings account. Their only income is Social Security of $600. Their monthly expenses are $600. A split decision can be made on this overpayment. Social Security can recover $900 to reduce their total assets to $5,000. The remaining $700 overpayment can be waived because reducing their assets below $5,000 will *defeat the purpose of Title II.*

Example 6: Bob and Dale were notified that they were over-paid $500. They claimed that they were without fault in causing the overpayment and unable to repay. The SSA learned that they still have the $500 in Social Security benefits deposited in a savings account. Recovery of the overpayment would not *defeat the purpose of Title II.* However, if they had used $300 to pay debts, this portion of the overpayment may justify the finding of *defeat the purpose of Title II.* They would still be responsible to repay the remaining $200.

Section 1108 Guidelines on Assets

If all your income is required for your support (see Sec. 1109), the Social Security Administration will look at your assets to decide if recovery of an overpayment would defeat the purpose of Title II. (see Sec. 1107.)

Generally, the SSA will not require you to reduce your assets below $3,000 to pay back an overpayment. If you have a dependent, the guideline is $5,000. You can allow an additional $600 for each additional dependent. For instance, the guideline for a person with two dependents is $5,600.

Assets include all liquid assets, such as bank accounts, stocks, bonds, etc., and the reasonable value of nonliquid assets, such as real estate. The following are *not* included:

- the value of household furnishings;

- apparel;

- burial plot or prepaid burial contract;

- the family automobile;

- the family home;

- a vehicle needed for the support of a handicapped family member (in order for a vehicle to meet this exclusion, it must provide support that the family vehicle cannot provide, and must have been purchased and be used for the transportation of the disabled person); and,

- any asset that is generating income needed to meet ordinary and necessary living expenses.

IRAs and Keogh Plan funds are not assets when the fund is income-producing; otherwise, they should be considered as assets.

If you are the beneficiary of a trust fund, it is an asset if you have access to the funds and they are liquid. If you own real estate jointly, your share is not an asset if the other owners do not agree to sell the property. Social Security does include assets resulting from a pending inheritance, even if not yet received.

Example 1: You are overpaid $2,500. You are without fault and you need all your income for your support. You have no dependent, but your assets are $4,000. Social Security will waive recovery of $1,500, but require repayment of $1,000, the amount by which your assets exceed the guidelines.

Example 2: Harry has assets over the guidelines. However, his wife is seriously ill. There are outstanding medical bills that, when paid, will reduce the assets below $5,000. More medical bills are anticipated that will soon wipe out the remaining assets. Harry's present assets will not preclude a finding of *defeat the purpose of Title II.*

Section 1109 Guidelines on Income and Expenses

To be eligible for waiver of an overpayment on the grounds that recovery would *defeat the purpose of Title II* (see Sec. 1107), you first must show that you need all of your income to meet your living expenses. If you receive public assistance, you will automatically meet this requirement. The Social Security Administration has flexibility when considering your income and expenses. They do not wish to cause a hardship. However, they will not accept expenditures that are beyond the ordinary and necessary living expenses for food, clothing, and shelter, taking into account your standard of living. But they will not allow expenses for a luxurious standard of living that developed after you received the overpaid money.

Income from all sources is counted, including the income of a spouse and other dependent relatives living in the same house, whether or not they receive benefits.

The amount of reasonable expenses depends on the cost of living for your area. The knowledge and judgment of the local SSA employee reviewing your case is considered. Expenses include those incurred for food, clothing, rent, mortgage payments, utilities, maintenance, life, accident and health insurance premiums, taxes, installment payments, medical and drug bills, child support, charitable contributions, newspapers, cigarettes, household supplies, gasoline, and other miscellaneous expenses. If a debt will be paid off in the near future, this will also be considered.

SOCIAL SECURITY TIP

Expenses to purchase or maintain nonessential items such as a boat or vacation home are not counted.

If your allegations about your living expenses, income, or assets appear incorrect, the SSA will require you to produce evidence to prove them. They will require verification if expenses appear too high, if the SSA interviewer doubts that the income and assets of other household members have been included, or if you received a large retroactive check that was an overpayment and you claim you no longer have the funds because of unusually large expenditures.

If your expenses are higher than your income, Social Security will want to know how you meet them. If you cannot produce evidence of this, such as a dwindling bank account, they will not believe you.

There are no hard and fast rules about the types of acceptable evidence. If evidence you first submit appears convincing, you will not be required to produce better evidence that may be available. Evidence that is commonly accepted includes letters from employers, copies of tax returns, tax receipts and bills, installment payment books, etc.

SECTION 1110 COMPROMISE SETTLEMENTS

The Social Security Administration has authority to accept compromise settlements when the amount of the overpayment is not greater than $20,000. This means that they may accept less than the total overpayment in full settlement. In that case, there will be no further recovery of the balance. An offer to settle an overpayment greater than $20,000 will be referred to the Justice Department or the General Accounting Office.

The SSA cannot compromise an overpayment claim if the overpayment resulted from fraud, unless the overpaid person is deceased and the overpayment is $5,000 or less. However, if someone else who is still alive contributed to the fraud, the claim cannot be compromised regardless of the amount.

A claim to recover an overpayment may be compromised only if one of the following conditions exists.

- You are unable to repay the full amount within a reasonable time or the government is unable to enforce collection within a reasonable time.

- There is real doubt about the government's ability to prove its case in court.

- The cost of collecting the claim is likely to exceed the amount of recovery (this is presumed if the difference between the compromise offer and the amount of the overpayment is less than $500).

A compromise offer must be in writing and signed by the overpaid person. An offer signed by an attorney may also be accepted if it appears the attorney is in a position to carry out its terms.

The written statement should include the following:

- the reason a lesser amount has been offered;

- the overpaid person's name, claim number (see Sec. 1407), and current address;

- the total amount of the overpayment;

- the amount offered as a compromise;

- when and how the compromise amount will be refunded (it should be within thirty days after acceptance of the offer); and,

- an understanding that if the compromise is not promptly paid, the full amount will be due.

Once the offer is made, it will take several months to get an answer. The decision whether to accept it is not made in the district office. It is referred to a Program Service Center or the Office of Disability Operations. (see Sec. 102.) If the SSA does not accept the offer, they may make a counter offer.

SECTION 1111 GUIDELINES FOR ACCEPTING COMPROMISE OFFERS

The Social Security Administration will first decide if it has authority to compromise if an offer is made. (see Sec. 1110.) If so, it will consider whether it could recover the overpayment by withholding checks within the next three months. If so, the offer to settle should be at least 80% of the total overpayment.

If enforced collection is not possible, an offer of 50% of the overpayment will usually be accepted if you are financially unable to repay in full. An offer of less than 50% may be accepted if you are financially unable to pay more than the amount offered.

If you are financially able to repay in full, but enforced collection is not possible, an offer of 60% will usually be accepted.

SOCIAL SECURITY TIP

These guidelines are not binding rules. The SSA has discretion to accept or reject any compromise offer. There are no appeal rights from a rejection of an offer to compromise.

If a request for waiver of overpayment (see Sec. 1104) or an appeal from the overpayment determination is pending, no action will be taken on the compromise offer until the outcome.

SECTION 1112 REPAYMENT

If you are not eligible for waiver of an overpayment (see Sec. 1104), and there is no compromise settlement (see Sec. 1110), the overpayment must be repaid. When the Social Security Administration notifies you that you are overpaid, they demand repayment in full.

If you are a beneficiary, they will tell you that your checks will be withheld until the overpayment is recovered in full. Nevertheless, Social Security will accept installments (see Sec. 1114) or impose only partial monthly deductions (see Sec. 1113) if you ask them.

No interest is charged on overpayments, no matter how long you take to repay. You may pay by credit card.

Section 1113 **Deductions**

The Social Security Administration may withhold your monthly benefits to recover an overpayment. They always propose to withhold benefits in full until the total amount is recovered. If you ask, however, they will usually agree to withhold only part of the monthly benefits. They will do this provided that the full overpayment will be recovered within twelve months, and the partial withholding is at least $10 per month.

If recovery by partial withholding for twelve months would cause a financial hardship, the SSA may extend the period, but no longer than thirty-six months. They will require financial information from you to explain the hardship. Interest is never charged on past-due amounts.

Section 1114 **Installments**

The Social Security Administration will accept repayment of an overpayment in monthly installments instead of deductions from your checks if you ask for this arrangement. The same rules that apply to partial monthly deductions (see Sec. 1112) also apply to installments.

MEDICARE  12

SECTION 1201 MEDICARE—IN GENERAL

Medicare is the health insurance program under the auspices of the Health Care Financing Administration, a branch of the Department of Health and Human Services. Medicare is no longer under the jurisdiction of the Social Security Administration, although the SSA is a primary source of information, applications, and claims for Medicare. All questions on

Medicare can be answered by contacting any Social Security office, or the toll-free number at:

800-MEDICARE

(800-633-4227)

The CMS website can be found at **www.cms.hhs.gov**.

Original Medicare is divided into two parts: *hospital insurance* (Part A) and *medical insurance* (Part B). In many areas of the country you may choose a Medicare Advantage Plan that allows you to participate in *Health Maintenance Organizations* (HMOs), *Preferred Provider Organizations* (PPOs) and other arrangements that may provide additional benefits and coverage, including prescription drug coverage. This is referred to as Part C. You may also enroll for drug coverage under the *Prescription Drug Coverage Plan* (Part D).

Under Part D you enroll directly with a private prescription drug provider company. You may select from hundreds of different plans depending on where you live, each providing different benefits. Under the law certain minimum coverage amounts must be provided. You apply to the insurance company and pay the monthly premium directly to the company, although you may have it deducted from your social security check in some plans.

If you have a low income and limited resources you may be eligible for subsidies for the premiums and deductible. Application for the low income assistance is made to the Social Security Administration.

Hospital insurance is financed through a portion of the FICA payroll deduction from the paychecks of workers. Medical insurance is partially financed through the collection of monthly premiums. These are either deducted from Social Security checks or paid directly by covered individuals. See Appendix 11 for the amount of the premiums.

Many private insurance companies also offer coverage of hospital and medical expenses that are not covered by Original Medicare Parts A and B. This is commonly called Medigap Coverage. This coverage does not work with Part C Medicare Advantage Plans.

SECTION 1202 HOSPITAL INSURANCE (PART A)

Hospital insurance pays for four basic areas of medical care:

- in-patient care in a hospital;

- medically necessary in-patient care in a skilled nursing facility immediately following hospitalization (most nursing homes are not skilled nursing facilities);

- home health care; and,

- hospice care.

All hospital insurance claims are paid on the basis of benefit periods. The first benefit period begins with the first hospitalization but ends sixty calendar days after the termination of Medicare services (hospitalization, a skilled nursing facility, or rehabilitation services). There is no limit to the number of benefit periods an individual can have under hospital insurance.

Medicare hospital insurance does not pay for the entire stay in the hospital. In each benefit period, Medicare pays for all covered services for the first through the sixtieth day, except for the average cost of one day's hospitalization. For the sixty-first through ninetieth day in the hospital, Medicare pays for all covered services except for one-quarter of the average cost of each day in the hospital. In addition, every Medicare beneficiary is entitled to sixty *lifetime reserve days*. For lifetime reserve days, Medicare pays for all covered services except for the cost of one-half of the average cost for each day in the hospital. See Appendix K for these co-payment amounts.

SECTION 1203 MEDICAL INSURANCE (PART B)

Medicare medical insurance pays for six basic areas of medical care:

1. doctor's services, both in his or her office and in the hospital;

2. outpatient hospital care;

3. outpatient physical and speech therapy;

4. home health care;

5. ambulances; and,

6. medically necessary durable medical equipment, such as wheelchairs.

All payments under Medicare medical insurance Part B are based on reasonable charges, not the current charges made by the physicians. Reasonable charges are determined by comparing the customary charge made by each doctor in the previous calendar year for each service with the prevailing rate for each service. The *prevailing rate* is the amount that will cover the customary charge in 75% percent of the bills submitted to Medicare in the previous year.

Medicare medical insurance pays 80% of the reasonable charge, after a predetermined deductible has been met, based on covered services (*i.e.*, what Medicare would have paid that may be different from the doctor's fee). All deductibles for Medicare Part B are based on the calendar year.

Medicare Part B also covers certain preventive screenings such as flu shots and cancer screenings. See Appendix L for a chart of services covered as of 2007.

Premiums

You must pay a monthly premium for Medical Insurance. (see Appendix K for the amount.) If you do not elect to be covered by Medical Insurance when you are first eligible, you can enroll only during a *general enrollment period*. (see Sec. 407.) If more than twelve months have passed since the close of your *initial enrollment period*, you must pay an extra 10% for each full twelve-month period beginning with the first month after the initial enrollment period and ending with the last month of the general enrollment period in which you apply.

Example: John turned age 65 and was otherwise eligible for Medicare medical insurance in January 2006, but he does not enroll for Part B until January 15, 2008, during a general enrollment period. His initial enrollment period closed April 2006, the third month after his 65th birthday. (see Sec. 407.) The months considered for the premium increase are May 2006 through March 2008. There are twenty-three months in this period, which is only one full twelve-month period. His monthly premium will be increased by 10% (rounded to the nearest 10¢).

For purposes of figuring the extra premium, you do not count any months during which you were covered both by Medicare hospital insurance (Part A) and an employer group health plan. (see Sec. 1204.)

Section 1203.1 **Prescription Drug Coverage (Part D)**

Prescription drug benefits under a program called Part D are covered by Medicare beginning in 2006. Drug benefit coverage you may have under other plans, such as through your employment or your spouse's employment, may be affected if you enroll in Part D. If you are covered by a Medicare Advantage Plan you must enroll in Part D through that plan. If you enroll in Part D through another plan you will be disenrolled from the Medicare Advantage Plan. Medigap plans—private plans other than Medicare Advantage Plans—will no longer cover drug benefits in the future. Incarcerated beneficiaries are not eligible for the Medicare Part D. If you become incarcerated after enrolling you will be disenrolled.

Under Part D, you buy drug coverage insurance from a private company that is approved by Medicare and agrees to provide certain minimum levels of coverage. The monthly premium is deducted from your social security check, electronically withdrawn from your bank account, or billed to you to pay. In exchange, Medicare subsidizes the costs the companies pay for the drugs. You have your choice of any plan that offers coverage in your region. There are 48 geographic versions of plan coverage. There are over one thousand different plans that offer different cover amounts for different drugs and work with different pharmacies, so it is important to choose a plan that will cover your particular drugs in your own area pharmacy.

It is virtually impossible to select the best plan for you without using a computer program that allows you to put in a list of your prescription drugs and the area where you live to compare the various premiums, deductibles and savings. This computer program is available on the internet at the Medicare website. Go to **www.medicare.gov** and look for the link that says "Compare Medicare Prescription Drug Plans." This will allow you to find and compare drug plans available in your area that provide the best benefits for the particular prescription drugs you take.

If you do not know how to use the Internet and cannot find someone who can help you, you can call Medicare or a state, government-run assistance office designed to help people through this process. Each state has set up an office for this purpose. See the chart below for the phone number of the office in your state.

Listing of Telephone Number for
State Health Insurance and Assistance Programs

ALABAMA
1-800-243-5463 Or
1-334-242-5743

ALASKA
1-800-478-6065 Or
1-907-269-3680

AMERICAN SAMOA
1-808-586-7299

ARIZONA
1-800-432-4040 (Az Only)
Or
1-602-542-6595 Or
1-602-241-6171

ARKANSAS
1-800-852-5494 Or
1-501-371-2785 Or
1-501-371-2782

CALIFORNIA
1-800-434-0222 (CA Only)
Or
1-916-323-7315

COLORADO
1-800-544-9181 Or
1-303-894-7499 (Ext. 356)

CONNECTICUT
1-800-994-9422

DELAWARE
1-800-336-9500 Or
1-302-739-6266

DISTRICT OF COLUMBIA
1-202-676-3900

FLORIDA
1-800-963-5337 Or
1-850-414-2060

GEORGIA
1-800-669-8387

GUAM
1-808-586-7299

HAWAII
1-808-586-7299

IDAHO
1-800-247-4422 (Boise)
1-800-488-5431 (Twin Falls)
1-800-488-5725 (Lewiston)
1-800-488-5764 (Pocatello)

ILLINOIS
1-800-548-9034 Or
1-217-233-3475

INDIANA
1-800-452-4800 Or
1-317-233-3475

IOWA
1-800-351-4664 Or
1-515-242-5190

KANSAS
1-800-860-5260 Or
1-316-337-7386

KENTUCKY
1-502-564-7372

LOUISIANA
1-800-259-5301 Or
1-504-342-0825 Or
1-225-342-5301

MAINE
1-800-750-5353

MARYLAND
1-800-243-3424 (MD Only)
1-410-767-1100
TTY: 1-410-767-1083

MASSACHUSETTS
1-800-882-2003

MICHIGAN
1-800-803-7174

MINNESOTA
1-800-803-7174

MISSISSIPPI
1-800-948-3090 Or
1-601-359-4956

MISSOURI
1-800-390-3330 Or
1-573-893-7900 (Ext. 137)

MONTANA
1-800-332-2272 (MT Only)
1-406-444-7781

NEBRASKA
1-402-471-2201

NEVADA
1-800-307-4444 Or
1-702-486-4602

NEW HAMPSHIRE
1-800-852-3388 Or
1-603-225-9000

NEW JERSEY
1-800-792-8820

NEW MEXICO
1-800-432-2080 Or
1-505-827-7640

NEW YORK
1-212-869-3850 (New York
City Only)
1-800-333-4114

NORTH CAROLINA
1-800-443-9354
1-919-733-0111

NORTH DAKOTA
1-701-328-2977
1-800-247-0560

NORTHERN MARIANA
ISLANDS
1-800-586-7299

OHIO
1-800-686-1578
1-614-644-3399

OKLAHOMA
1-800-763-2828
1-405-521-6628

OREGON
1-800-722-4134
1-503-947-7984

PENNSYLVANIA
1-800-783-7067
1-717-783-8975

PUERTO RICO
1-787-721-8590
1-800-981-4355

RHODE ISLAND
1-800-322-2880
1-401-222-2880

SOUTH CAROLINA
1-800-868-9095
1-803-253-6177

SOUTH DAKOTA
1-800-822-8804
1-605-773-3656 (Pierre)
1-605-336-2475 (Sioux Falls)
1-605-342-3494 (Rapid City)

TENNESSEE
1-800-525-2816
1-615-242-0438

TEXAS
1-800-252-9240

UTAH
1-800-439-3805
1-801-538-3910

VERMONT
In State: 800-642-5119
Out Of State: 802-748-5182

VIRGINIA
1-800-552-3402
1-804-662-9333

VIRGIN ISLANDS
1-809-778-6311 Ext. 2338

WASHINGTON
1-800-397-4422
1-360-407-0383

WEST VIRGINIA
1-304-558-3317
1-800-642-9004

WISCONSIN
1-800-242-1060
1-608-267-3201

WYOMING
1-800-856-4398
1-307-856-6880

SOCIAL SECURITY TIP

All questions regarding enrollment or choosing a prescription drug plan should be made to the state office in your state or to 1-800-MEDICARE. All questions regarding premiums should be referred to the drug plan insurance company. Do not call the Social Security Administration with questions about premiums because they will refer you to Medicare or the insurance company. However, you should call Social Security for low income assistance for the Part D premiums and copays discussed below.

If you enroll in Part D you pay a small monthly premium, which varies by plan, and a yearly deductible, which also varies by plan and changes from year to year – between $0 - $265 in 2007, to $275 in 2008. You also pay a copayment or coinsurance, which again varies by plan. Then Medicare pays 75% of the costs between the deductible and the initial benefit limit, $2,400 (2007) or $2510 (2008) in drug spending. You pay 25% of these costs. You pay 100% of the drug costs above $2,250 until you reach the catastrophic threshold of $3,850 (in 2007) or $4,050 (in 2008) in out-of-pocket spending. This level between the initial benefit limit and the *catastrophic threshold* is called a coverage gap, or *donut hole*. Some drug plans may offer options to help you pay the out-of-pocket costs.

After you have spent the required out-of-pocket amount, Medicare will pay about 95% of the costs. This is referred to as *catastrophic coverage*. The approximately 5% you pay is through copayments and coinsurance. You will pay $2.15 in 2007 and $2.25 in 2008 for a generic or preferred drug and $5.35 in 2007 and $5.60 in 2008 for other drugs, or a flat 5% coinsurance – whichever is greater. The out-of-pocket amount is paid annually. You must reach the out-of-pocket threshold each year.

For updated information for future years you can go to: www.SocialSecurityBenefitsHandbook.com.

SOCIAL SECURITY TIP

If you have low income and limited assets you may receive subsidies. If you qualify, you will only pay a small copayment for each prescription, and you may also get help paying the premiums and the deductible. Low income means less than 150% of the *federal poverty level*. For 2007, this was $15,315 for a single person household and $20,535 for a two person family, adding $5,220 to the limit for each additional person in the family. The amounts are somewhat higher in Alaska and Hawaii. You may qualify for extra help if your combined savings, investments, and real estate - not counting your home - are worth less than $11,710 if you are single, or $23,410 if you are living with your spouse. These amounts change each year. The rules are complex and cannot be discussed fully here. You should call Social Security to apply for a subsidy so that you may not have to pay a premium or deductible. Call Social Security at 1-800-772-1213 (TTY 1-800-325-0778) or visit the website at **www.socialsecurity.gov** to apply online. The Social Security Administration handles the applications for Part D low income subsidies.

Section 1203.2 **Part D Enrollment Periods**

All enrollments in Part D are processed by the plan companies rather than by Social Security. You may enroll when you first become eligible for Medicare during the Initial Enrollment Period for Part B (see Sec. 407), and each year after that from November 15 - December 31, called the *annual enrollment period*. There are also *special enrollment periods* if you lose employer-based coverage, move from the drug insurance company's service area, or if it goes out of business or is decertified by Medicare.

If you apply when you are first eligible for Medicare your coverage will be effective the month after the application is given to the drug insurance company, but not before Medicare begins. If you miss you first enrollment period and apply during the annual enrollment period (November 15-December 31), then coverage is effective January of the following year. If you apply during a special enrollment period, coverage will be effective in the month after the month the enrollment form is completed. If you are eligible for both Medicaid and Medicare, coverage will be effective the month the application is given to the insurance company.

If you do not enroll when first eligible and you do not have *creditable prescription drug coverage*—a drug plan that provides at least as good coverage as Part D—or you do not qualify for a special enrollment period, you are subject to a penalty.

Examples of creditable coverage may include:

- Coverage under a prescription drug plan or Medicare Advantage plan with prescription drug coverage

- Medicaid

- Group Health Plan (GHP)

- State Pharmaceutical Assistance Program

- VA coverage

- Medigap with prescription drug coverage

- Military service related coverage including TRICARE

If your creditable drug coverage ends, you have to enroll in Part D within 63 days to avoid the late enrollment penalty fees.

The late fee is 1% of the National base premium – $27.35 for 2007, for a penalty of $0.27 per month – for each month after May 2006 for which you are eligible for Part D but are not enrolled. This penalty fee is a permanent increase to the premium.

You may change to another plan once a year without penalty during the annual enrollment period with the change being effective January 1st of the following year. You may want to change coverage plans if the drugs you need change or you move to a different area. The plans may also change their copays and premiums from year to year, as well as which drugs are available under the plan.

SOCIAL SECURITY TIP

Even if you do not need coverage because you have not been prescribed drugs, you may want to enroll in a plan that has a very small premium. This way, if you need expensive prescription drugs in the future you will be able to switch over to a better plan without paying a late-filing penalty.

For years after 2007, beneficiaries who are eligible for the low income subsidy will be responsible for a portion of late fees as well.

NOTE: *If you are eligible for a low-income subsidy you may enroll at any time in 2007 without a penalty.*

Section 1204 Private Health Insurance

Medicare is designed to provide basic protection against the very high cost of health care, but it will never pay all of your medical expenses. Because of this, many private insurance companies offer different protection in their policies. You should shop and compare different companies to determine which policy would be best for you.

For example, if you need several prescriptions, perhaps a company that covers prescription costs would be more advantageous. Other plans may offer eyeglass or dental plans. There is no single supplemental health plan that is best for everybody.

If you are over age 65 and you (or your spouse) work for an employer who has twenty or more employees, your employer is required to offer you the same health insurance benefits offered to younger workers. If you continue working after age 65, you have a choice of either accepting or rejecting your employer's health plan. If you accept it, Medicare will become a secondary health insurance plan for you, and your employer's health plan would be the primary insurance plan (the first payer). If you drop Part B because you are covered by the private plan, you may reenroll when the private coverage ends. (see Sec. 407.)

You have the option of rejecting your employer's health plan, and if you do, Medicare will become your primary health insurance plan.

SECTION 1205 WHAT IS NOT COVERED

Medicare hospital insurance pays for all routine care in a hospital, including a semiprivate room, all your meals, regular nursing service, lab tests, and x-rays. It does not cover other items that are purely for personal convenience, such as the television, a radio, or a telephone. It will not pay the charge for private duty nurses or extra charges for a private room unless it is determined to be medically necessary, for example, to isolate a contagious disease.

Medicare *medical insurance* will not pay for the following services:

- routine physical examinations and tests related to routine physical examination, other than preventative services (see Sec. 1203);

- routine foot care;

- eye or hearing examinations for prescribing or fitting eyeglasses or hearing aids (Medicare will pay for some eye services related to cataract surgery);

- immunizations other than flu shots and some other types of vaccination (see Sec. 1203);

- most cosmetic surgery; and,

- most dental care (dental care will be covered only if it involves surgery of the jaw or the setting of fractures of the jaw or facial bones).

SOCIAL SECURITY TIP

For a comprehensive list of what is or is not covered by Medicare, obtain a copy of the *Medicare Handbook* published by the Social Security Administration, or visit the Medicare website at **www.medicare.gov**.

SECTION 1206 ASSIGNMENT OF BENEFITS

Assignment of benefits is a procedure by which the doctor agrees to accept direct payment from Medicare for services provided to you. If a doctor accepts an assignment, he or she agrees to accept the amount that Medicare approves as full payment for the service. Medicare would then pay 80% of that amount. You are still responsible to pay the 20% that Medicare does not pay.

SECTION 1207 WHEN TO FILE CLAIMS

Virtually all services rendered by hospitals and skilled nursing facilities are submitted directly to Medicare by the hospital. They will receive payment directly. You will receive only a notice of how much was paid and what the covered services are.

Some physicians, whether or not they accept assignment, will forward the claim for reimbursement to Medicare. If the physician does forward the claim to Medicare and has accepted assignment, you will receive an explanation of how much money was paid to the physician.

If the physician does not accept assignment, you will receive an explanation of how much Medicare pays along with a check.

You may forward your bills to Medicare as soon as you receive them or you may save and submit them all at once. Since many people have a tendency to save their bills until the deductible is met or to save up their bills for the entire year and submit them all at once, the last three months of the year and the first three months of the year are very busy for Medicare and may result in a substantially longer time to process your request for reimbursement.

SOCIAL SECURITY TIP

It is generally advisable to submit your Medicare claims on a *flow* basis. As soon as you receive the service, submit the bill.

SECTION 1208 PROCESSING OF CLAIMS

Claims for Medicare medical insurance benefits are not processed by either the Social Security Administration or the Health Care Financing Administration. These are processed by various private health insurance companies throughout the country. These companies are known as Medicare carriers.

Example: All Medicare Part B claims for services provided by doctors in Alabama will be forwarded to Medicare Blue Cross/Blue Shield of Alabama in Birmingham.

Claims in the State of Hawaii are sent to Medicare Aetna Life and Casualty Company in Honolulu.

You are told who your carrier is when you become entitled to Medicare. If you do forward the Medicare claim to the wrong office, that office will forward it to the correct one.

Section 1209 Medicare Card

Everyone entitled to Medicare hospital insurance or medical insurance is issued a red, white, and blue card that is entitled *Health Insurance Social Security Act*. This is known as the *Medicare card*. The information on the card includes your name, your Social Security claim number, and your sex. It indicates whether you are entitled to hospital insurance benefits only, medical insurance benefits only, or both. It also shows the effective date.

You are issued only one Medicare card and it is good for as long as you are entitled. The SSA will issue replacements only if your card is lost or stolen. It normally takes about four to six weeks after your initial application for Medicare is processed to receive the card. If you need to use Medicare before you receive it, the Social Security office can issue you a temporary letter of eligibility that will contain the information on the Medicare card.

Appeals Process 13

Section 1301 Appeals—In General

Social Security regulations establish an appeals process that must be followed if you wish to appeal a decision regarding your case. Not every administrative action may be appealed. (see Sec. 1302.) The appeals process has different levels—reconsideration, hearing, and Appeals Council review. You must go through this process before a federal court will review your case.

You have the right to be represented by an attorney at any stage in your dealings with the Social Security Administration (SSA). This is not usually necessary unless you have a problem. You should be represented if you go to the hearing stage of the appeals process. An attorney may charge you a fee if the amount has been approved by the SSA. (see Sec. 1310.)

The legal rules of evidence do not apply in these administrative proceedings. This means you may submit any evidence you wish, even if it is not admissible in a court of law.

Section 1302 What You Can and Cannot Appeal

You can appeal only an *initial determination*. This is a formal decision affecting benefits, a period of disability, your earnings record, or entitlement to Medicare. Claims for payment under medical insurance (Medicare Part B) are not reviewed by the Social Security Administration. Disputes about such payments are reviewed by the insurance company that administers medical insurance in your state. These cases cannot be reviewed in federal court.

Initial determinations include:

- awards or disallowances of monthly benefit claims;

- computations and recomputations of monthly benefit amounts;

- decisions on deductions from benefits and termination of benefits;

- *representative payee* determinations (see Sec. 1414);

- overpayment decisions; and,

- determinations about your earnings record.

Whenever an initial determination is made concerning your case, you will receive a written notice. This may be an award certificate, a disallowance letter, or a letter explaining the decision. The date of this letter starts the time limit for a request for a reconsideration. (see Sec. 1308.)

Administrative decisions that are not initial determinations include:

- payment of combined checks (see Sec. 1004);

- withholding of part of a monthly benefit to recover an overpayment; and,

- authorizing the amount of an attorney's fee.

Any administrative action that is not an initial determination cannot be appealed through the normal appeals process and is not reviewable in court.

SECTION 1303 RECONSIDERATION

The first step in the administrative appeals process is the *reconsideration*. You or your representative, such as an attorney, may request it. The request may also be filed by another person whose benefit rights are adversely affected by a determination made in your case.

You do not have to fill out the forms yourself. The claims representative will do this for you, but you or your representative must sign them.

If you are appealing a disability denial, you should bring with you the names and addresses of all your treating doctors and hospitals. Be prepared to describe in detail any change in your condition and how it affects your daily activities.

You may submit any evidence you wish. Copies of medical reports and hospital records will be accepted, unless they appear to be altered. The Social Security Administration will not request evidence for you.

SOCIAL SECURITY TIP

The reconsideration is a review of your record by a member of a different staff from the one that made the initial determination.

The request for a reconsideration must be filed within sixty days of the notice of the initial determination. (see Sec. 1308.)

SECTION 1304 PERSONAL CONFERENCE— OVERPAYMENT CASES

If your appeal is from a denial of your request for waiver of an overpayment (see Chapter 11), you may have a *personal conference* instead of a reconsideration. The personal conference is usually conducted by a claims representative at your local district office. You may appear (with an attorney if you wish) and explain your case. Any evidence you wish to submit will be considered.

The personal conference must be requested within sixty days of the notice of the initial determination. (see Sec. 1308.)

SECTION 1305 **HEARING**

The *hearing* is the single most important step in the appeals process. It is conducted by an *administrative law judge* (ALJ). The ALJ will independently review your case on the basis of the evidence in the file, any evidence you submit, and your sworn testimony. You may appear in person and be represented by an attorney. It is extremely important to have your attorney present. The proceedings will be recorded on a tape recorder, not by a stenographer. A hearing assistant may be present to operate the recording system.

The administrative law judge may arrange for the testimony of expert witnesses called on behalf of the government. Vocational experts are frequently utilized in disability cases. You may produce your own experts to testify, but you are responsible for any fees. You may also request the ALJ to issue subpoenas requiring the attendance and testimony of witnesses or the production of documents or other evidence. Any such request for subpoenas should be made as far in advance of the hearing as possible (and no less than five days).

Notice of the time and place of the hearing is sent to you at least ten days in advance. If you have a lawyer, call him or her as soon as you receive your notice to make sure he or she has received one.

In disability cases it is very important for you to appear in person. The judge will ask you about your limitations, your medical treatments and medications, your work background, and your daily activities, among other things.

You must be fully prepared to answer these questions. Before the hearing, your lawyer and you will go over the questions you may be asked.

Be as specific and complete as possible in your answers, but never exaggerate. The judge will be looking for this. You should be able to describe how much weight, in pounds, you are able to lift and carry; how long you can sit, stand, and walk; and whether you have limitations bending, climbing, pushing, or pulling.

If you suffer from pain, be prepared to describe it as sharp or dull, its frequency and location, what activities produce or aggravate it, and what relieves it. You should describe any side effects from medication, such as drowsiness, nausea, or impaired concentration.

The hearing will usually last about an hour. If you wish to submit additional evidence, you may request the judge to hold the record open for a week or two.

The judge will make a written decision on your case within a month after the hearing. If you win, you will receive benefits about a month later.

The request for hearing must be filed within sixty days of the reconsideration denial. (see Sec. 1308.) Your hearing will be scheduled within two or three months.

Section 1306 **Appeals Council Review**

You may request review of the administrative law judge's decision within sixty days after the decision is made. The Appeals Council may also review the decision of its own initiative within the same time.

The Appeals Council may deny your request for review, which it does in most cases. If so, the decision of the administrative law judge is the final decision of the SSA.

If the Appeals Council believes that a significant question of law or policy is involved in your case, it may grant review. In some cases it may allow you or your lawyer to appear before it in Washington, D.C., and present oral arguments. The Appeals Council then will make its decision, which is final.

Sometimes cases are referred back to the administrative law judge to obtain additional evidence. This is called a *remand*. The ALJ will make another decision that again may be reviewed by the Appeals Council.

Section 1307 **Court Review**

The Social Security Act provides that a federal district court has the authority to review any final decision of the Social Security Administration if it was rendered after a hearing. This means you must go through the administrative appeals process before going to court. After the district court reviews your case, it can affirm, reverse, or send it back to the SSA for further proceedings (also known as *remand*).

The court's review is limited to determining if the decision is supported by substantial evidence or contains an error of law. If there is any evidence to support the decision, you will lose, unless there is a legal error. For example, if the administrative law judge chose to give more weight to one doctor's report (saying you are not disabled) than to another doctor's report (saying you are disabled), the court likely will uphold the decision. The ALJ is considered the *fact-finder* and his or her conclusions will not be disturbed if supported by more than a *scintilla of evidence* (*i.e.*, such evidence as a reasonable mind might accept as adequate to support a conclusion).

If there is error in the ALJ's application of the law to the facts of your case, the court may overturn the decision. Such cases may result in a remand to the administrative law judge to determine additional facts in light of the correct rule of law.

A legal action seeking review of a final decision must be filed in federal district court within sixty days. The court's filing fee is currently $60. Any legal fees must be approved by the court.

SECTION 1308 **TIME LIMITS**

A request for a reconsideration, hearing, or Appeals Council review must be filed within sixty days of the prior decision. The time limit for filing a civil action in federal court is the same.

SOCIAL SECURITY TIP

The time starts running from the date you receive the notice of the decision. This is presumed to be five days after the notice was mailed.

A protective filing statement (see Sec. 402) will stop the running of the time limit for administrative appeals, but not for the civil action. It must indicate clearly an intent to appeal. No formal words are required, simply: *I wish to appeal the decision in my case.*

The time limit for requesting an administrative review may be extended if you had *good cause* for late filing—for example, if you were hospitalized or if you never received the notice of the decision. The time limit for filing a civil action may be extended by the Appeals Council. A request for extension should be filed before the time limit expires. If not, the request may be granted if you had good cause for being late. If a time limit expires on a Saturday, Sunday, legal holiday, or a federal nonwork day, the time limit is extended to the next following work day.

SECTION 1309 REOPENING CLOSED CASES

A decision that has become final may be reopened and revised for any reason within twelve months of the notice of the initial determination.

A *decision* may be reopened within four years if one of the following conditions is met:

- new evidence is found after the initial determination;

- a clerical error was made in figuring a benefit amount;

- the initial determination was clearly wrong based on the evidence in file; or,

- there is good cause.

Good cause does not exist where the only basis for reopening is a change of legal interpretation.

A *determination* may be reopened at any time if one of the following conditions is met:

- fraud or similar fault was involved;

- someone else makes a conflicting claim on the same earnings record;

- the worker was presumed dead and is found alive or is now presumed dead because of unexplained absence for seven years (for survivor's benefits);

- a worker's earnings record now shows that a previous denial for insufficient earnings was wrong;

- an unfavorable decision was based on a clerical error apparent on the face of the evidence in file; or,

- errors were made involving railroad employment or military wage credits causing duplicate payments or the failure to give proper credit.

SECTION 1310 **ATTORNEYS**

Usually you will not require an attorney to handle your Social Security affairs, although you have the right to be represented at any time. Your case may require an attorney if your claim has been denied or you have incurred a substantial overpayment.

SOCIAL SECURITY TIP

Business owners who plan to claim retirement benefits should consult an attorney before they give any statements to the Social Security Administration. (see Sec. 811.)

If you wish to consult or retain a lawyer, it is important to find one well versed in the area of Social Security law. Few lawyers practice in this field, although the number is growing. The bar association in your county may be able to refer you to a suitable lawyer. Many lawyers who practice workers' compensation law also handle Social Security cases (especially disability).

You are responsible for the payment of your attorney's fee. However, any fee for services rendered representing you must be approved by the Social Security Administration.

If you win your case, the SSA will withhold 25% of any past-due benefits until an approved fee has been established. Most lawyers will accept a disability case on a contingent basis. This means that no fee will be charged if the case is unsuccessful.

When a fee has been approved, the SSA will pay the attorney directly out of the withheld benefits. If there is any unused balance, it will be sent to you. If the approved fee is greater than the amount withheld, the lawyer will bill you.

Sometimes an attorney may require you to pay a retainer in advance. If so, he or she must hold this in escrow (set apart from his or her own funds) until a fee has been approved. If the approved fee is less, he or she must return the difference to you.

MISCELLANEOUS PROVISIONS 14

Section 1401 Supplemental Security Income

Supplemental Security Income (SSI) cash payments are payable to the aged (65 and over), blind, and disabled (including children) who are in financial need. Social Security is an insurance program. SSI is a welfare program. It is mentioned only because it is administered by the Social Security Administration. This book does not go into the numerous rules, requirements, procedures, and details, as this program is beyond the scope of this book.

Entitlement to SSI is contingent upon the amount and types of income and resources you have available to you. The income and resources of those relatives legally responsible for your support (*e.g.*, parents of minor children, spouses) will also affect your entitlement to SSI.

The amount of the SSI payment is fixed for all recipients (although many states make supplemental payments included in the SSI check), but is affected by various factors, such as types and amounts of other income you receive, the value of your resources, and whether you live alone, with others, in a nursing home, or in a group home.

The SSI check is gold colored and is delivered on the first day of the month. Although the SSI program is administered by the Social Security Administration, the SSI payments do not come from the Social Security trust fund. The payments are made from the general revenues of the federal government derived from various tax payments. If you think you are eligible for SSI or require more information, you should contact your local Social Security office.

Section 1402 Black Lung Benefits

The federal Coal Mine Health and Safety Act of 1969 established payments to coal miners who suffer from pneumoconiosis, commonly referred to as *Black Lung*. Only Black Lung claims filed before July 1, 1973, are under the jurisdiction of the Social Security Administration. All applications filed after that date are under the jurisdiction of the Department of Labor. The SSA does maintain jurisdiction of claims filed by the survivors of miners who were afflicted with Black Lung.

Black Lung payments are made to coal miners who are totally disabled due to pneumoconiosis. Additional payments may be made to these miners to provide for a dependent wife, divorced wife, or children. Survivor benefits may be paid to widows, children, a surviving divorced wife, parent, brother, or sister of a miner who was entitled to Black Lung benefits at the time of his or her death, who was totally disabled by pneumoconiosis at the time of death, or who died from pneumoconiosis. For further information, contact the SSA or the Department of Labor.

Section 1403 Benefit Estimates

The Social Security Administration will provide an estimate of the amount of benefits payable to anyone who requests it. All benefit estimates given will be based on the amount of earnings actually shown on the record of earnings and will not be based on any proposed future earnings. Although the SSA will provide estimates for people of any age, those estimates for workers who are under age 60 cannot be completely accurate. Estimates for people of any age can only be based on the information currently available to Social Security. Estimates of benefits far into the future have been shown to be inaccurate because of changes in the Social Security Act and wide swings in inflation.

SOCIAL SECURITY TIP

If you are nearing retirement age and would like an estimate, you may contact your Social Security office or call 800-772-1213.

SECTION 1404 OBTAINING YOUR EARNINGS RECORD

The Social Security Administration will provide, free of charge, a *Statement of Earnings*. This statement shows the annual earnings credited to your record. Because of the amount of time it takes to process reports of earnings, the first and second year preceding the request may not be available. It is a good idea to check your Social Security records every three years.

SECTION 1405 CORRECTING YOUR EARNINGS RECORD

Usually, the earnings record can only be corrected up to three years, three months, and fifteen days after the year the wages were paid or self-employment income was earned. If you have a disagreement with your employer about how much you were paid, when you were paid, or whether the work was covered under Social Security, you must act within the three-year, three-month, fifteen-day time limit. If a disagreement exists, the SSA will help you obtain the necessary information to settle the dispute. Based on all evidence received, the SSA will decide whether earnings can be credited, how much earnings should be credited, and for what period. Social Security will notify you of the decision they have reached and what corrective action, if any, they are taking.

Once the three-year, three-month, fifteen-day time limit has expired, the earnings record cannot be revised unless one of the following conditions is met:

- an entry was established through fraud;

- a mechanical, clerical, or other obvious error is detected (such as earnings mistakenly reported under a wrong Social Security number or mistakenly unreported);

- earnings were credited to the wrong person or to the wrong period;

- transfer earnings to or from the Railroad Retirement Board were reported to the wrong agency;

- addition of wages paid by an employer who made no report of any wages paid to an employee;

- addition or removal of wages in accordance with a wage report filed by an employer;

- addition of self-employment income if the tax return was filed within the legal time limit; or,

- self-employment income up to the amount of employee wages deleted were erroneously reported if a self-employment tax return is filed within three years, three months, and fifteen days of the year the earnings were deleted. (This may occur where *employment* later is determined to be *self-employment*.)

The Social Security Administration does its best to ensure that wages are properly reported. Although corrections legally can be made at a later time, the longer you wait to correct a problem, the harder it will be because of destruction and loss of records. Take action to correct your Social Security record as soon as a problem is identified.

SECTION 1406 REPORTING CHANGE OF ADDRESS

A change of address can be reported to the Social Security Administration (SSA) using three methods—with a telephone call, visiting the office, or by letter.

The Department of the Treasury prepares and mails all government checks. The SSA must notify the Treasury Department of all address changes. Social Security checks are delivered to the local post offices well in advance of the due date to ensure their timely delivery. All of these factors take time. It can require as much as forty to forty-five days for a change of address to take effect. It is important to notify the SSA as soon as you know your new address. It is also important to file a change of address form with the post office so that even if the change of address does not register, the post office will forward your check.

Section 1407 Claim Numbers and Beneficiary Identification Codes

Every person who applies for Social Security benefits is assigned a claim number and all records are maintained by that number. The claim number consists of the Social Security number of the worker on whose account the benefits are based with a letter (or letter and number) following it. It is used on all correspondence from the Social Security Administration.

The retirement beneficiary's claim number is his or her Social Security number followed by the letter *A*. His or her spouse on the account is assigned his number followed by the letter *B* (if he or she is 62 or over) or *B2* (if he or she receives because he or she has a child in care). Children are identified by the letter *C* and a number (usually 1 for the youngest, 2 for the next youngest, etc.). Widow(er)s receiving on account of age are identified by the letter *D*.

If a person is entitled on more than one account, the records are maintained under both accounts, but one account takes precedence. If a widow(er) receives benefits both as a retired wage earner and as a widow(er), all correspondence and checks will be sent to him or her in his or her own number followed by the letter *A*. Other than the initial award letter, the secondary account number will not be mentioned. Beneficiary identification code letters are listed at Appendix H.

Section 1408 Who Gets Benefits Due a Deceased Beneficiary

An underpayment exists when benefits are due that have not been paid. Usually underpayments are due because of returned checks or increases in benefit amounts for various reasons. If the underpaid person is alive, the payment is made to him or her (or the person's representative).

A deceased person can also be due an underpayment. When this occurs, the underpayment is paid to whichever person is highest in priority in the following list.

1. To the widow or widower if she or he was living in the same household at the time of death, or, even if not, was entitled to monthly benefits on the same earnings record (receiving spouse's benefits—not including divorced spouse's benefits).

2. To the child(ren) of the underpaid person who was entitled to monthly benefits on the same earnings record as the deceased for the month of death. The underpayment is divided equally among all such children.

3. To the parent(s) of the underpaid person entitled to monthly benefits on the same earnings record for the month of death.

4. To the widow(er) who was neither living with the underpaid person nor entitled to monthly benefits on the same earnings record.

5. To the child(ren) who were not entitled to monthly benefits on the same earnings record as the deceased for the month of death.

6. To the parent(s) who were not entitled to monthly benefits on the same account as the deceased.

7. To the legal representative of the estate.

Example: If the deceased was survived by his wife who was living with him but not entitled to monthly Social Security benefits and an 18-year-old daughter who was receiving monthly Social Security benefits on his account, the underpayment would be paid to his widow. If the deceased and his wife were separated, the underpayment would be paid to his daughter. If the daughter was not entitled to monthly benefits and no one else was, the underpayment would be payable to the widow.

The underpayment is not paid to all persons on the list of priority. It is paid only to the highest person on the list. Two or more people with the same priority (*e.g.,* two surviving children) split the underpayment equally.

If the Social Security Administration can determine who is entitled to the underpayment, it will pay it automatically without a specific request. If the Social Security records are insufficient to determine all persons who may be entitled (surviving wife or children not entitled to monthly benefits) a request is required from one person who is entitled to share in the underpayment. Proof of relationship may be required.

SECTION 1409 TAXATION OF SOCIAL SECURITY BENEFITS

Social Security benefits are subject to income tax if you have income that exceeds the following amounts:

- $25,000, if you file as a single taxpayer;

- $32,000, if you are married and file a joint return; but,

- $0, if you are married and you live with your spouse at any time during the year and file separate returns.

When you figure your total Social Security benefits received, you have to include gross benefits before deductions for items such as the Medicare premium, a lawyer's fee, or workers' compensation offsets.

In figuring your total income, you must also include *nontaxable* earnings, such as interest from municipal bonds. The Social Security benefits are taxable only to the extent they exceed the above limits; however, for an individual, only 50% of the excess is taxable up to $34,000, 85% of the excess over $34,000. For a couple, 50% of the excess over $32,000 up to $44,000, then 85% of the excess over $44,000 is taxable.

If you wish, you may request that taxes be withheld from your benefits. To have your taxes withheld, you must complete IRS Form W-4V, called a Voluntary Withholding Request form. You may select what percentage of your monthly benefit amount you want withheld (either 7%, 15%, 28% or 31%—only these percentages can be used). Flat dollar amounts are not acceptable. After you have made your selection, sign and return the form to your local Social Security office by mail or in person.

SECTION 1410 IMMUNITY OF BENEFITS FROM CREDITORS

No creditor has the right to attach a Social Security benefit, except that benefits can be attached for child support or alimony payments or by the IRS for the payment of back taxes. Once the benefit has been received and put into an account such as a savings account or a checking account, it can be attached unless it is a separate account clearly marked *Social Security Benefits*. It is very important if you are receiving benefits on behalf of a child and placing them in a savings account that clearly specifies that the funds are Social Security funds, so that your creditors cannot attach the child's money.

SECTION 1411 CRIMINAL PENALTIES FOR FRAUD

Under the Social Security program, fraud can be found if a person furnishes false identity information to get a Social Security number, if a person furnishes a false statement in connection with a claim for Social Security benefits, or if a person uses a Social Security number obtained by fraud.

Fraud can also be found if a person conceals or fails to report any event affecting the right of a person to receive a Social Security check or uses Social Security benefits received on behalf of one person for the use of somebody other than that person. The Social Security Administration may prosecute fraud even if no benefits were ever paid by the government on the basis of the statement.

The penalty for fraud ranges from a minimum of not more than a $500 fine, or imprisonment of one year, or both to a fine of not more than $10,000, or imprisonment for up to fifteen years, or both. Acts such as alleging you retired when you actually have not or alleging that you transferred a business to your spouse when you did not are a few examples of cases Social Security may prosecute.

Section 1411.1 **Administrative Sanctions**

Even if criminal fraud is not involved or in addition to criminal fraud penalties, the Social Security Administration may impose sanctions when an individual makes (or causes to be made) a statement of a material fact to get benefits if:

- the statement is false, misleading, or omits a material fact;

- the person knows or should know the statement is false, misleading, or omits a material fact; and,

- the statement is made with a knowing disregard for the truth.

The sanction penalty is nonpayment of benefits for six months for the first occurrence, twelve months for the second occurrence, or twenty-four months for each occurrence after that. If the beneficiary is not currently receiving benefits, the penalties will be noted on the record and will be imposed if the person becomes entitled in the future.

SOCIAL SECURITY TIP

Only the guilty beneficiary will suffer sanctions—others receiving benefits on the account will not be subject to the sanction if they were without fault.

SECTION 1412 FOREIGN SOCIAL SECURITY CREDITS

The Social Security Administration has entered into international agreements, called totalization agreements, with twenty-one foreign countries. An agreement is pending with Mexico and must be approved by Congress. These countries include:

- Australia;
- Austria;
- Belgium;
- Canada;
- Chile;
- Finland;
- France;
- Germany;
- Greece;
- Ireland;

- Italy;

- Japan;

- Korea;

- Luxembourg;

- Netherlands;

- Norway;

- Portugal;

- Spain;

- Sweden;

- Switzerland; and,

- the United Kingdom.

The agreements allow people who have work credits in those countries to file an application with Social Security in the United States for potential Social Security benefits from the other country. This provision allows some people who do not have enough work under either Social Security system to be able to collect one Social Security benefit. It also allows people who are entitled to benefits from both systems to file for them and collect them conveniently.

At the time you file for Social Security benefits in the United States, the interviewer will ask if you ever worked in a foreign country covered by the agreement. The SSA will complete a second application for potential benefits from that other country for you.

SECTION 1413 **RAILROAD EMPLOYMENT**

People who work for the railroads are not covered under Social Security. They are covered by the *Railroad Retirement Board* (RRB). If you are entitled to benefits from both Social Security and from the RRB, they are made in one combined payment. The SSA will compute your Social Security benefit and send the information to the RRB, who will figure your annuity and adjust it for the amount of Social Security you receive.

To be entitled to railroad retirement benefits, an employee must have ten years of railroad service. With less than ten years of railroad service, the railroad employment will be credited to his or her Social Security account. If an employee does not have enough work to collect a Social Security payment, his or her earnings under Social Security will be credited to his or her railroad retirement account. Survivor benefits may be paid by either agency.

More information on railroad retirement benefits can be obtained by contacting Railroad Retirement Board field offices in major cities throughout the country or calling 800-808-0772.

Section 1414 Receiving Benefits for Someone Else—The Representative Payee

Social Security benefits will be paid to an adult in his or her own name unless he or she has been shown to be incompetent or incapable of managing his or her own funds. If a mentally ill person is still able to manage benefits in his or her own interest, the payment will be made directly to that person. A physically disabled person will have payments made to a representative payee only if so disabled as to be unable to manage benefit payments even with the help of someone else.

Benefits to children under the age of 18 normally are made to a representative payee. The payment may be made directly to a child under the age of 18 if the child is entirely self-supporting and living away from home or in other limited circumstances. It is unusual for a child under the age of 18 to collect payments on his or her own behalf. Benefits may not be paid to a child under age 15. Once a child turns age 18, payments are made directly, unless there is a need for a representative payee.

The order of preference in appointing a representative payee for a child is:

- a natural or adoptive parent with custody;

- a legal guardian;

- a natural or adoptive parent without custody, but who shows strong concern;

- a relative or stepparent with custody;

- a close friend with custody who provides for the child's needs;

- a relative or close friend without custody, but who shows strong concern;

- an authorized social agency or custodial institution; or,

- anyone not listed here who shows strong concern for the child, is qualified, is able to act as payee, and who is willing to do so.

The order of preference for an adult is:

- a spouse, parent, or other relative with custody or who shows strong concern;

- a legal guardian with custody or who shows strong concern;

- a friend with custody;

- a public or nonprofit agency or institution;

- a federal or state institution;

- a statutory guardian;

- a voluntary conservator;

- a private, for-profit institution with custody and is licensed under state law;

- a friend or relative without custody, but who shows strong concern for the beneficiary's well being;

- an organization that charges a fee for its service; or,

- anyone not listed here who is qualified and able to act as payee, and who is willing to do so.

The responsibilities of a representative payee are:

- to apply benefit payments for the beneficiary's use;

- to maintain a concern for the personal welfare of the beneficiary;

- to notify the SSA when the responsibility for the welfare and care of any person entitled to Social Security ends;

- to report to the SSA any changes that may affect the beneficiary's right to receive Social Security; and,

- to give the SSA periodic written reports accounting for the use of benefits, if requested to do so.

Benefits paid to a representative payee must be spent for the beneficiary's current needs or saved for the beneficiary if all current needs are being met.

If you receive Social Security benefits on behalf of another and find that you are able to save some to establish a bank account for the person, the bank account must clearly indicate that the funds in that account are Social Security benefits. The preferred format for the title of the account is: "Name of Beneficiary, By Name of Representative Payee" or "Name of Beneficiary, By Name of Representative Payee, Trustee." A bank account title such as "Name of Payee in Trust for Beneficiary" should not be used because some states treat the funds in such an account as belonging to the representative payee. Whatever the title of the account is, it must clearly indicate that the money in the account is the property of the beneficiary and no one else, and that it is derived from Social Security benefits.

The Social Security Administration requires a written account from representative payees on a periodic basis. If you are acting as a representative payee, you should keep records showing how the Social Security money was spent. The reporting you will be asked for may include the amount of benefits you had at the beginning of the period, where the beneficiary lived during the period, the amount of income from other sources during the year, how the benefits were spent, how much of the Social Security benefits were saved, and how they were invested.

LIST OF SECONDARY PROOF OF AGE

(see Sec. 410)

If no birth certificate or baptismal certificate recorded before age 5 is available, the Social Security Administration requires you to submit other documents to prove age. This appendix identifies documents that can be used to prove age. The information is divided into two sections—*First Priority Convincing Records* and *Second Priority Convincing Records*.

I - First Priority Convincing Records

If you submit one document from the list and the date of birth on that document agrees with the date of birth you gave the Social Security Administration when you applied for your Social Security number, no other proof of age is necessary.

I-1. Family Bible or other family record recorded before age 36.

I-2. School or school census records recorded before age 21.

I-3. 1910, 1920, or 1930 federal census record.

I-4. Domestic or Canadian delayed birth record established before age 55.

I-5. State census records for 1905 or 1915.

I-6. Insurance policies taken out before age 21.

I-7. Immigration and Naturalization Service (INS) arrival records recorded before age 31.

I-8. Religious records recorded before age 18.

I-9. Newspaper birth announcements.

II - Second Priority Convincing Records

If no First Priority Convincing Record is available (as well as no birth or baptismal record recorded before age 5), you should submit one document from this list. If the date of birth on that document agrees with the date of birth you gave the Social Security Administration when you applied for your Social Security number, no other proof of age is necessary.

II-1. School records recorded after age 20 and before age 55.

II-2. Baptismal record recorded after age 17 and before age 55.

II-3. 1925 state census records.

II-4. Domestic or Canadian delayed birth record established after age 54—if the delayed birth record shows the basis for the date of birth.

II-5. Birth records for your children recorded before you were age 31.

II-6. Marriage records recorded before age 36.

II-7. Citizenship data recorded before age 26.

II-8. World War II draft and discharge records recorded before age 31.

II-9. Employment records established before age 21.

II-10. Voting records established before age 56.

II-11. Other records recorded before age 21.

QUARTERS OF COVERAGE REQUIRED FOR INSURED STATUS

Following is a chart showing the earnings required for a *quarter of coverage* and four charts that show the minimum number of quarters of coverage needed for Insured Status, according to the type of benefit.

Chart 1: Earnings Required for a Quarter of Coverage

Year	Amount
Pre-1978	$ 50
1978	250
1979	260
1980	290
1981	310
1982	340
1983	370
1984	390
1985	410
1986	440
1987	460
1988	470

1989	500
1990	520
1991	540
1992	570
1993	590
1994	620
1995	630
1996	640
1997	670
1998	700
1999	740
2000	780
2001	830
2002	970
2003	890
2004	900
2005	920
2006	970
2007	1,000

(If you have access to the Internet, you may check online at **www.socialsecuritybenefitshandbook.com** for later years.)

Chart 2: Number of Quarters Required for Insured Status for Disability or Survivor Benefits

(For People Born in 1930 or Later)

Age of Onset of Disability or Death Required	Minimum Number of Quarters of Coverage
28 and younger	6
29	7
30	8
31	9
32	10
33	11
34	12
35	13
36	14
37	15
38	16
39	17
40	18
41	19
42	20
43	21
44	22
45	23
46	24
47	25
48	26
49	27
50	28
51	29
52	30

53	31
54	32
55	33
56	34
57	35
58	36
59	37
60	38
61	39
62 and older	40

Chart 3: Disability Insured Status

(see Sec. 604)

NOTE: *This chart shows the minimum number of quarters of coverage required in the calendar quarters immediately preceding onset of disability. For example, 15/30 means that 15 quarters of coverage are needed in the 30 calendar quarters (7½ years) before onset of disability; 20/40 means that 20 quarters of coverage are needed in the 40 calendar quarters before onset of disability (10 years).*

Age at Onset of Disability	Minimum Number of Quarters of Coverage Required/Calendar Quarters Before Disability
24 and younger	6/12
24½	7/14
25	8/16
25½	9/18
26	10/20
26½	11/22
27	12/24
27½	13/26
28	14/28
28½	15/30
29	16/32
29½	17/34
30	18/36
30½	19/38
31	20/40

APPENDIX C
LIST OF FICA
YEARLY MAXIMUMS

(Maximum Earnings Subject to Social Security Tax)

Year	Earnings
1937 through 1950	$ 3,000
1951 through 1954	3,600
1955 through 1958	4,200
1959 through 1965	4,800
1966 through 1967	6,600
1968 through 1971	7,800
1972	9,000
1973	10,800
1974	13,200
1975	14,100
1976	15,300
1977	16,500
1978	17,700
1979	22,900
1980	25,900
1981	29,700
1982	32,400
1983	35,700
1984	37,800

1985	39,600
1986	42,000
1987	43,800
1988	45,000
1989	48,000
1990	51,300
1991	53,400
1992	55,500
1993	57,600
1994	60,600
1995	61,200
1996	62,700
1997	65,400
1998	68,400
1999	72,600
2000	76,200
2001	80,400
2002	84,900
2003	87,000
2004	87,900
2005	90,000
2006	94,200
2007	97,500

Future maximums will be increased based on the rate of inflation and announced by the Social Security Administration in the fall of the preceding year. (If you have access to the Internet, you may check online at **www.socialsecuritybenefitshandbook.com** for updated information.)

APPENDIX D
SAMPLE BENEFIT AMOUNTS

*Worker with steady earnings at the **maximum** level since age 22*

Retirement at Beginning of Year	Retirement at Age 62	Retirement at Full Retirement Age	Retirement at Age 70
	Monthly Benefit	Monthly Benefit	Monthly Benefit
2000	$1,248	$1,433	$1,751
2001	$1,314	$1,536	$1,877
2002	$1,382	$1,660	$1,988
2003	$1,412	$1,721	$2,045
2004	$1,422	$1,784	$2,111
2005	$1,452	$1,874	$2,252
2006	$1,530	$1,961	$2,420
2007	$1,598	$1,998	$2,672

(Check online at **www.socialsecuritybenefitshandbook.com** for later years.)

*Worker with steady earnings at the **high** level since age 22*

Retirement at Beginning of Year	Retirement at Age 62	Retirement at Full Retirement Age	Retirement at Age 70
	Monthly Benefit	Monthly Benefit	Monthly Benefit
2000	$1,115	$1,279	$1,553
2001	$1,169	$1,364	$1,658
2002	$1,224	$1,467	$1,747
2003	$1,242	$1,512	$1,785
2004	$1,245	$1,559	$1,831

(Check online at **www.socialsecuritybenefitshandbook.com** for later years.)

*Worker with steady earnings at the **average** level since age 22*

Retirement at Beginning of Year	Retirement at Age 62	Retirement at Full Retirement Age	Retirement at Age 70
	Monthly Benefit	Monthly Benefit	Monthly Benefit
2000	$858	$987	$1,212
2001	$897	$1,051	$1,291
2002	$935	$1,126	$1,357
2003	$947	$1,157	$1,386
2004	$947	$1,190	$1,420

(Check online at **www.socialsecuritybenefitshandbook.com** for later years.)

*Worker with steady earnings at the **low** level since age 22*

Retirement at Beginning of Year	Retirement at Age 62	Retirement at Full Retirement Age	Retirement at Age 70
	Monthly Benefit	Monthly Benefit	Monthly Benefit
2000	$521	$598	$729
2001	$544	$636	$776
2002	$568	$682	$815
2003	$575	$701	$922
2004	$575	$721	$852

(Check online at **www.socialsecuritybenefitshandbook.com** for later years.)

REDUCTION FACTORS

(see Sec. 703)

The full retirement age (*i.e.*, the age at which one may receive an unreduced retirement, spouse's, or widow's benefit) has been increased effective with those born in 1938 and later (1940 for widows) on a gradually increasing basis. (See Sec. 703 *Reductions* for a full discussion.) Therefore, additional reduction months are applied to those turning 62 (60 for widows) in 2000. For retirement and spouse's benefits, the reduction factor for reduction months in excess of 36 is $\frac{5}{12}$ of 1 percent for each extra month.

Chart 1: Retirement Benefits

Reduction Months	Reduction Factor	Reduction Months	Reduction Factor	Reduction Months	Reduction Factor
1	.994	13	.927	25	.861
2	.988	14	.922	26	.855
3	.983	15	.916	27	.850
4	.977	16	.911	28	.844
5	.972	17	.905	29	.838
6	.966	18	.900	30	.833
7	.961	19	.894	31	.827
8	.955	20	.888	32	.822
9	.950	21	.883	33	.816
10	.944	22	.877	34	.811
11	.938	23	.872	35	.805
12	.933	24	.866	36	.800

Chart 2: Spouse's Benefits

Reduction Months	Reduction Factor	Reduction Months	Reduction Factor	Reduction Months	Reduction Factor
1	.993	13	.909	25	.826
2	.986	14	.902	26	.819
3	.979	15	.895	27	.812
4	.972	16	.888	28	.805
5	.965	17	.881	29	.798
6	.958	18	.875	30	.791
7	.951	19	.868	31	.784
8	.944	20	.861	32	.777
9	.937	21	.854	33	.770
10	.930	22	.847	34	.763
11	.923	23	.840	35	.756
12	.916	24	.833	36	.750

Chart 3: Widow(er)'s Benefits

Unlike retirement and spouse's benefits, the widow(er)'s reduction is limited to 28.5%. This requires a different fraction depending on the year of attainment of full retirement age (FRA). For widow(er)s, the primary insurance benefit is reduced by a fraction of the PIA for each reduction month according to the following chart.

Date of Birth	FRA	FRACTION
Through 1/1/40	65	$\frac{19}{40}$
1/2/40 – 1/1/41	65 + 2	$\frac{57}{124}$
1/2/41 – 1/1/42	65 + 4	$\frac{57}{128}$
1/2/42 – 1/1/43	65 + 6	$\frac{19}{44}$
1/2/43 – 1/1/44	65 + 8	$\frac{57}{136}$
1/2/44 – 1/1/45	65 + 10	$\frac{57}{140}$
1/2/45 – 1/1/57	66	$\frac{19}{48}$
1/2/57 – 1/1/58	66 + 2	$\frac{57}{148}$
1/2/58 – 1/1/59	66 + 4	$\frac{57}{152}$
1/2/59 – 1/1/60	66 + 6	$\frac{19}{52}$
1/2/60 – 1/1/61	66 + 8	$\frac{57}{160}$
1/2/61 – 1/1/62	66 + 10	$\frac{57}{164}$
1/2/62 or later	67	$\frac{19}{56}$

Appendix F
Cost of Living
Increases

Cost-of-Living Allowance (COLA) increases are applicable for benefits paid in the year indicated in the chart. The effective month of COLA increases is December of the year preceding, and the increase affects benefits payable beginning January of the indicated year.

Year	Percentage
1992	3.7%
1993	3.0%
1994	2.6%
1995	2.8%
1996	2.6%
1997	2.9%
1998	2.1%
1999	1.31%
2000	2.4%
2001	2.6%
2002	1.4%
2003	2.1%
2005	2.7%
2006	4.1%
2007	3.3%

(If you have access to the Internet, you may check online at www.socialsecuritybenefitshandbook.com for later years.)

EARNINGS LIMITS
BY YEAR

Full retirement age (FRA), the age at which you may receive an unreduced benefit, has been increased. For retirement and spouse's benefits, the increase applies to those born in 1938 and later. For widow(er)'s benefits, the increase applies to those born in 1940 or later. Full retirement age goes up on a gradually increasing basis. (see Sec. 703.) The charts in Sec. 703 show the full retirement age based on the year of birth. Earnings after FRA do not cause a reduction in benefits.

Year	Age	Monthly	Yearly
2000	Under FRA	840	10,080
	FRA	1,416	17,000
2001	Under FRA	890	10,680
	FRA	2,083	25,000
2002	Under FRA	940	11,280
	FRA	2,500	30,000
2003	Under FRA	960	11,520
	FRA	2,560	30,720
2004	Under FRA	970	11,640
	FRA	2,590	31,080

Year	Age	Monthly	Yearly
2005	Under FRA	1,000	12,000
	FRA	2,650	31,800
2006	Under FRA	1,040	12,480
	FRA	2,770	33,240
2007	Under FRA	1,080	12,960
	FRA	2,870	34,440

(Check online at **www.socialsecuritybenefitshandbook.com** for later years.)

APPENDIX H
MOST COMMON BENEFICIARY IDENTIFICATION CODES

A: Retirement on Own Work Record
B: Aged Wife
B1:   Aged Husband
B2:   Young Wife (with Child in Care)
B6:   Divorced Wife
C: Child
D: Aged Widow
D1:   Aged Widower
D6:   Surviving Divorced Wife
E: Young Widow (mother)
E1:   Surviving Divorced Mother
E4:   Young Widower (father)
F: Parent
G: Lump Sum Claimant
HA: Disabled Worker
HB: Aged Wife of Disabled Worker
HB2:   Young Wife of Disabled Worker
HC: Child of Disabled Worker
J: Prouty (special age 72 benefits)
K: Prouty (wife)
M: Medicare—Medical Insurance Only

T: Medicare Only—Both Parts
W: Disabled Widow
W1:   Disabled Widower
W6:   Surviving Disabled Divorced Wife

Appendix I
Chart Summarizing the Effect Between Beneficiaries

(see Sec. 904)

Type of Beneficiary	Effect of Marriage to Another Beneficiary
Type I	
Retired Worker (see Sec. 202)	No effect, benefits continue.
Disabled Worker (see Sec. 203)	
Widow(er) (see Sec. 204.4)	
Disabled Widow(er) (see Sec. 204.6)	
Surviving Divorced Spouse (divorced widow(er)) (see Sec. 204.7)	
Disabled Surviving Divorced Spouse (divorced widow(er)) (see Sec. 204.7)	
Type II	
Divorced Spouse (see Sec. 204.3)	Benefits terminate if marriage is to a retired or disabled worker, or a child under 18 or in school; if marriage is to any other beneficiary, benefits continue.
Parent (see Sec. 206)	

Type III

Mother/Father (young widow(er)) (see Sec. 204.5)	Benefits terminate if marriage to a child under 18 or in school (child's benefits also terminate); if marriage is to any other beneficiary, benefits continue.
Divorced Mother/Father (see Sec. 204.7)	
Disabled Adult Child (see Sec. 213)	

Type IV

Child under 18 or in School (see Secs. 205.1–205.2)	Benefits terminate upon remarriage to anyone.

Appendix J
Delayed
Retirement Credits

The amount of a *delayed retirement credit* is calculated as a percentage of the primary insurance amount, based on the number of months no benefit is received after full retirement age. The percentages listed are annual. The credit for each month is ¹⁄₁₂ of the annual figure. The amount of the credit is based on year of birth.

Year of Birth	Annual Credit
1917–24	3%
1925–26	3.5%
1927–28	4.0%
1929–30	4.5%
1931–32	5%
1933–34	5.5%
1935–36	6%
1937–38	6.5%
1939–40	7.0%
1941–42	7.5%
1943 and later	8.0%

MEDICARE PREMIUMS
AND DEDUCTIBLES
FOR 2007

Hospital Insurance
  Premium—Part A

Free if you have 40 quarters of coverage.
$226/mo if you have 30-39 quarters.
$410/mo if you have less than 30 quarters.

Hospital Insurance—Part A

Co-Payments
  First 60 Days (Total) $992
  61st-90th Day (per day) $248
  Lifetime Reserve (per day) $496

Skilled Nursing Care
  20-100th day (per day) $124

Medical Insurance
  Premium—Part B

Beginning in 2007, this premium is based on income according to the chart on page 342.

You Pay	If Your Yearly Income is	
	Single	*Married Couple*
$93.50	$80,000 or less	$160,000 or less
$105.80	$80,001-$100,000	$160,001-$200,000
$124.40	$100,001-$150,000	$200,001-$300,000
$142.90	$150,001-$200,000	$300,001-$400,000
$161.40	Above $200,000	Above $400,000

You Pay	If You Are Married but You File a Separate Tax Return From Your Spouse and Your Yearly Income is
$93.50	Under $80,000 or less
$142.90	$80,001-$120,000
$161.40	Above $120,000

Medical Insurance—Part B
Yearly Deductible $131

(Check online at **www.socialsecuritybenefitshandbook.com** for later years.)

Appendix L

Preventative Services Covered by Medicare Part B as of 2007

The chart in this appendix lists the preventative services covered by Medicare Part B as of 2007, who and what is covered, and whether coinsurance or a deductible is involved.

Service	Who and What is Covered	How Often is it Covered	Coinsurance or Deductible
Flu Injection	Anyone with Medicare	Once per flu season, or more frequently if medically necessary	None
Pneumococcal Injection	Anyone with Medicare	Once in a lifetime	None
Hepatitis B Injection	Anyone with Medicare who is deemed to be at medium to high risk	One series if ordered by a physician	Coinsurance and deductible
Initial preventive physical exam (*i.e.,* the *Welcome to Medicare* physical exam)	All new enrollees in Medicare Part B may receive an exam that includes medical and social history review, a physical examination, and an electrocardiogram (ECG), with counseling, referral, and a written plan for additional preventive services that are needed. NEW – In 2007, anyone with Medicare who is at risk for abdominal aortic aneurysms may get a referral for a one-time screening ultrasound at their initial physical examination.	One time within the first six months you have Medicare Part B.	Coinsurance and deductible. You pay 20% of the Medicare-approved amount with no Part B deductible for the abdominal aortic ultrasound screening.
Cardiovascular disease screening	Anyone with Medicare Part B may receive an assessment of his or her blood lipid levels.	Every five years	None
Diabetes screening	Anyone with Medicare who has two or more of the following qualifications: is age 65 or older, is overweight, has a family history of diabetes, has a history of gestational diabetes, or has delivered a baby weighing more than nine pounds. Those with Medicare who have high blood pressure, dyslipidemia, obesity, or a history of high blood sugar may receive a test for elevated blood glucose.	One screening per year if you were never previously tested or if you were previously tested but did not get diagnosed with pre-diabetes. Two screenings per year if you have been diagnosed with pre-diabetes.	None

Service	Who and What is Covered	How Often is it Covered	Coinsurance or Deductible
Pap test and pelvic screening exams	Women with Medicare who are age 40 or older	Once every twelve months.	Coinsurance. No deductible.
Screening mammograms	Women with Medicare who are age 40 or older	Once every twelve months	Coinsurance. No deductible
	Women with Medicare who are age 35-39	One baseline mammogram	
Colorectal cancer screening	Anyone with Medicare who are age 50 or older. There is no minimum age for a screening colonoscopy or barium enema as an alternative to colonoscopy.	Fecal occult blood tests once every twelve months. Flexible sigmoidoscopy every 48 months or once every 120 months after having a screening colonoscopy. Screening colonoscopy every 24 months if you at high risk. If you are not at high risk, then every 120 months. Barium enema every 24 months if you are at high risk. If you are not at high risk, then every 48 months.	None for fecal occult blood tests. For all other tests, then coinsurance and deductible. NEW: Starting in 2007, Medicare will waive the Part B deductible for the colorectal screening benefit. Coinsurances will still apply.
Prostate cancer screening	Men with Medicare who are over the age of 50.	Digital rectal exam once every twelve months. Prostate Specific Antigen (PSA) Test once every twelve months.	Coinsurance and deductible for digital rectal exam. None for PSA Test.
Bone mass measurements	Anyone with Medicare whose doctor says they are at risk for osteoporosis	Every 24 months or more often if deemed to be medically necessary.	Coinsurance and deductible
Glaucoma tests	Anyone with Medicare who has diabetes, a family history of glaucoma, is African American and age 50 or older, or is Hispanic and age 65 and over	Once every twelve months	Coinsurance and deductible

345

INDEX

ABOUT THE
AUTHOR

Stanley A. Tomkiel, III is a practicing attorney and a partner with his son in the New York law firm of Tomkiel & Tomkiel, with offices in Bronxville and Manhattan. He is admitted to practice law in New York and in Florida. Tomkiel & Tomkiel is listed in the Bar Register of Preeminent Lawyers.

Before practicing law, Mr. Tomkiel was a claims representative for the Social Security Administration and worked in several offices in the Northeast, including New Jersey, Connecticut, and Massachusetts. After becoming an attorney, he handled Social Security disability claims on behalf of disabled claimants for many years. He now is available as a consultant to professionals, including lawyers, accountants, and financial planners dealing with Social Security issues.

He lectures at continuing legal education seminars and is a member of numerous professional associations. Mr. Tomkiel has achieved the highest rating—AV—by Martindale-Hubbell, which indicates very high to preeminent legal ability and very high ethical standards as established by confidential opinions from members of the bar.

Mr. Tomkiel received his Bachelor of Arts in English from Manhattan College, Bronx, N.Y., and his Juris Doctor law degree from Western New England College, School of Law, Springfield, Massachusetts. He is married and the father of two children.